KU-351-100

Baking

Baking

Hannah Baskerville

hamlyn

Published in the UK in 1997
by Hamlyn, a division of Octopus Publishing Group Ltd
2–4 Heron Quays, London E14 4JP

This edition published 2001

Copyright © 1997, 2001 Octopus Publishing Group Limited

ISBN 0 600 60574 4

Printed in China

All rights reserved. No part of this publication may be
reproduced, stored in a retrieval system or transmitted in
any form or by any means, electronic, mechanical,
photocopying, recording or otherwise, without the
permission of the publisher.

NOTES

Both metric and imperial measurements have been given in
all recipes. Use one set of measurements only and not a
mixture of both.

Standard level spoon measurements are used in all recipes.
1 tablespoon = one 15 ml spoon
1 teaspoon = one 5 ml spoon

Eggs should be medium to large unless otherwise stated.
The Department of Health advises that eggs should not be
consumed raw. This book contains dishes made with raw or
lightly cooked eggs. It is prudent for more vulnerable people
such as pregnant and nursing mothers, invalids, the elderly,
babies and young children to avoid uncooked or lightly cooked
dishes made with eggs. Once prepared, these dishes should
be refrigerated and used promptly.

Milk should be full fat unless otherwise stated.

Measurements for canned food have been given as a standard
metric equivalent.

Nuts and nut derivatives
This book includes dishes made with nuts and nut derivatives.
It is advisable for customers with known allergic reactions to
nuts and nut derivatives and those who may be potentially
vulnerable to these allergies, such as pregnant and nursing
mothers, invalids, the elderly, babies and children, to avoid
dishes made with nuts and nut oils. It is also prudent to
check the labels of pre-prepared ingredients for the possible
inclusion of nut derivatives.

Vegetarians should look for the 'V' symbol on a cheese to
ensure it is made with vegetarian rennet. There are vegetarian
forms of Parmesan, Feta, Cheddar, Cheshire, Red Leicester,
dolcelatte and many goats' cheeses, among others.

Ovens should be preheated to the specified temperature
– if using a fan-assisted oven, follow the manufacturer's
instructions for adjusting the time and the temperature.

Contents

Introduction

There's nothing like the appetizing aroma of freshly baked bread or cakes, the sheer pleasure – and indulgence – of eating the richest of fruit cakes or the lightest of sponges, of serving a home-made cake for a special family celebration, or crisp little biscuits to accompany a special dessert.

Sadly, baking has an old-fashioned image, dating from the days when women spent long hours in the kitchen preparing food in laborious and time-consuming ways. But it isn't like that any more; there simply isn't the time. This book is about baking the modern way – about making baking easy. Fortunately, the modern cook doesn't have to blanch and grind nuts, beat mixtures by hand or wait long hours for the butter to soften.

Mrs Beeton would envy us, for nowadays much of the hard work is done before we even start to knead the dough. Yeast is now readily available in fresh and easy-blend varieties designed to rise faster than ever before. Flour is graded, labelled and sold in easily identifiable bags for pastry, bread or cakes, and there are as many different kinds of nuts – toasted, ground or chopped as you wish – in every good supermarket.

There is also an exciting range of new ingredients, such as sesame, sunflower and pumpkin seeds, to give the dough a real lift. Pistachio and cashew nuts are available all the year round, and there is a wide choice of exotic dried fruits, from cranberries and blueberries to mangoes – all sold washed and ready to use – to add extra flavour to cakes.

That's why baking is in fashion; it is easier than ever before – and the results are even more impressive. It is also part of the current trend for good food and drink with real rather than synthetic flavours. This book shows how to achieve the maximum results with the minimum effort. It's quick, it's easy and, above all, it's fun.

USEFUL EQUIPMENT

You don't need a lot of specialist equipment for baking. However, a hand-held whisk, ideally an electric one, is invaluable for cake batters, whipping cream and beating icings. A food processor is useful, but not essential, for making scones and shortbread and it saves a lot of time.

Good strong tins are important and, luckily, many supermarkets now offer a wide range. You can't go wrong with a basic loaf tin, a 20 cm/8 inch round cake tin, a Swiss roll tin, a basic bun tin, a couple of sandwich tins and a sturdy baking sheet for making biscuits. The most convenient tins to use have a non-stick lining and a detachable base.

To get the best results choose a tin as close to the size given in the recipe as you can. If the tin is larger, the cake mixture will be spread in a thinner layer and cook more quickly; if it is smaller the depth of the mixture will be increased and take longer to cook. A square tin holds approximately the same quantity of mixture as a round tin which measures 2.5 cm/1 inch larger in diameter than the side of the square tin if they are of the same depth. That means an 18 cm/7 inch square tin has the same capacity as a 20 cm/8 inch round tin. You will find that exquisite little tins for making tiny bread rolls – such as mini loaf tins and flowerpot moulds – are great fun, and very tempting, but not essential.

You will, though, need a good set of biscuit cutters. A perspex rolling pin is extremely useful for rolling out fondant moulding paste and marzipan. A piping bag and nozzle are useful but if you can't pipe, don't worry. Only a few recipes in this book are designed for the serious cake decorator. If you find you need a piece of equipment that you don't have at home – the horseshoe-shaped tin for the Anniversary Cake on page 79, for example – don't buy it; hire it instead. Cream horn moulds are worth buying, however, and cost very little.

BASIC HINTS AND TIPS

• Always preheat the oven before you start. Most ovens don't heat up immediately whatever claims their manufacturers make, and many a cake has sunk because the oven wasn't hot enough.

• Ground spices will not keep their flavour for much longer than a year and then only if they are kept in airtight, light-proof containers. Ideally, buy spices unground and write the purchase date on the container.

• Before you start, check whether or not you need to prepare the tin. It is a nightmare when you are halfway through a recipe, particularly if you've spent ages whisking air into a sponge, to have to stop suddenly and spend time greasing and flouring a tin.

• The best way to grease a tin is to melt a little butter or lard and brush it over the tin. Then, if the recipe calls for the tin to be coated with flour, simply roll flour around the base and sides of the tin (as with the Whisked Sponge on page 41).

• A 'greased and lined tin' is one which has been buttered (or larded) and then the base and sides lined with greaseproof paper. If you are making a Christmas cake, or any other cake which takes a long time to cook, you will find it useful to put a double layer of greaseproof or brown paper around the outside of the tin to stop the sides from over-browning and drying out.

• Always make sure you weigh out and have ready all the ingredients before you start a recipe. That way, you will know you actually have everything you need and won't waste time chopping fruit while the cake batter is sitting around losing valuable air.

• To make a successful whisked sponge, make sure you really do whisk the eggs and sugar thoroughly. The best way to check is to lift the whisks out of the mixture and write a 'W' with the cake batter. If the 'W' stays in the batter for 8 seconds, then the mixture is stiff enough.

• When you are making cakes and biscuits, it's worth having the butter at room temperature before you start. The best way to achieve this quickly is to put it in the microwave, on high, for a couple of seconds.

• Adding the flour to biscuit mixtures can be done with a beating motion, but it is very important with cake batters to fold in the flour gently, using a large metal spoon, otherwise the cake will toughen.

• It is easier to turn a cake out of the tin on to a wire cooling rack if you place the rack on the tin, hold the tin and rack with a cloth and turn both over together.

• When you are making a novelty cake, knead the colouring into the icing and then ignore any disturbances. If you leave the fondant moulding paste rolled out on a work surface while you answer the phone, for example, you will find it is much too dry to mould over the cake.

• If you have never piped decorations before, then don't start with a cake for a special occasion. There are many other ways of making cakes look special – such as using a silk or chiffon ribbon. Coloured edible ink pens are excellent for marking the top of the cake (see the Pony Cake on page 82). And you can buy ready coloured icing which saves a lot of fiddling around getting the right colour (you could use it for the Aeroplane Cake on pages 80–81, if you like).

• To decorate a cake quickly without icing, place a large paper or plastic doily over the top of the cake and dredge the cake heavily with sifted icing sugar, then carefully remove the doily and you will have an attractive pattern underneath.

• If you realize too late that you have no icing sugar to sift over a cake, grind granulated sugar in a coffee grinder or food processor and use this instead.

Stretching the dough: This is part of the kneading process and helps give a good rise and even texture to the finished loaf.

Punching the dough: Before rising, the dough is stretched and punched until it feels firm, elastic and smooth. This takes about 10 minutes.

Unrisen dough: All yeast doughs must rise once – sometimes twice – before baking, before and after shaping, to allow the yeast to work.

MAKING BREAD

Making bread is really very easy. Make sure you follow the instructions carefully for adding fresh or easy-blend yeast and make sure the water you use is tepid. If it is too hot it will kill the yeast and if it is too cold the yeast won't activate.

Knead the dough carefully. This strengthens the dough and ensures that it rises properly. Use the heel of your hand and stretch the dough away from you. Give the dough a quarter turn and repeat the stretching, punching and folding. Continue for 10 minutes. Imagine the dough is someone you hate – it's a splendid way of getting rid of aggression.

Once the dough has been kneaded for 10 minutes it is important to give it time to relax and prove. Simply cover it with oiled clingfilm and put it in a warm, but not hot, place until it has doubled in size. This will take about an hour.

When the dough has doubled in size, then it is knocked back. This means kneading the dough with your knuckles to get rid of any remaining air bubbles and to give it an even texture.

Shape the dough into the prepared tin, cover with oiled clingfilm and leave to prove until it has, once again, doubled in size.

It's important to cover the dough while it is rising, otherwise it develops a tough skin. Make sure that bread always goes into a very hot oven – it is usually 220° F (425°C), Gas Mark 7 or 230°F (450°C), Gas Mark 8. The hot oven kills the yeast.

To check when the bread is cooked, turn it out of the tin and tap the bottom of the loaf. If it sounds hollow, then it is cooked.

COMMON MISTAKES

A loaf with a sour or bitter taste means that the yeast was not fresh enough or the dough was over-proved. A lack of volume and an uneven texture mean that either the dough was under-kneaded or under-proved or the oven was too hot. On the other hand, a lack of volume and an open crumbly texture mean that the dough was over-proved or the oven not hot enough. A flying top, when the top crust breaks away from the loaf, happens because the dough was not kneaded until elastic, or under-proved, so that the crust bakes hard before the loaf expands.

MAKING CAKES

Depending whether they are made with high, medium or low quantities of sugar, fat, flour and eggs, cakes are usually described as being rich, plain

Risen dough: Rising time varies according to the temperature and quantity of dough and yeast. For the best bread, dough should always be allowed to rise slowly.

or sponge and are mostly made by one of four basic methods.

Rich cakes, those made with equal quantities of fat and sugar – such as Madeira Cake (see page 44), Victoria Sandwich Cake (see page 37) and the Christmas Cake on page 74, all use the creaming method where the fat is blended or creamed with the sugar.

Plain cakes, so called because they contain a ratio of up to half fat to flour, are made by the rubbing-in method, where the fat is rubbed into the flour with the fingertips. This is the method used for the Little Cakes on page 91.

Sponge cakes may be made without fat but contain a high proportion of sugar and eggs, which are whisked until they are almost white before the

Knocking back the dough: This is a short second kneading to knock the air bubbles out of the risen dough and make it ready for shaping.

flour is folded into the mixture. Fatless sponges should be eaten fresh as they dry out quickly. A Genoese Sponge (see page 40) is a whisked sponge enriched with melted butter; it is richer than a fatless sponge and keeps better. An Angel Cake (see page 38) is a whisked sponge made without butter and using only the whites of eggs.

Finally, there are recipes made by the melted method, such as the Sticky Gingerbread on page 47, in which the fat and sugar are melted before they are added to the dry ingredients.

Biscuits, whether simple like Langues de Chat (see page 50) or slightly more complicated like French Honey and Almond Biscuits, a type of petit four (see page 69), are made in the same way as cakes. It is always a good idea to bake one or two trial biscuits to see how much they spread during baking. You can then space them suitably on the baking sheets.

Proving the dough: After shaping, the dough is then given a second rising (or proving). This takes about 10–15 minutes in a warm kitchen.

FREEZING BREAD AND CAKES

Most breads and rolls will freeze satisfactorily after baking. They should be cooled quickly, then wrapped tightly in foil or heavy polythene and frozen at once. Plain loaves can be frozen for up to 6 months and should be thawed completely before use.

Many cakes freeze well too, although it is often best to add the icing after the cake has thawed. Butter cream freezes very well and cakes either filled or topped with this should be packed in a rigid container for protection. An un-iced cake can be wrapped in foil or thick polythene or put into a rigid container. Individual cakes can be frozen in polythene bags or rigid containers and can be open frozen first, if liked. Plain cakes can be stored for 6–9 months in the freezer but highly spiced ones are best used within 2 months, and individual cakes should not kept for too long.

Breads

Basic White Bread Dough

750 g/1½ lb strong white or unbleached flour	450 ml/¾ pint water
2 teaspoons salt	or 1½ teaspoons dried yeast with 1 teaspoon
15 g/½ oz lard	caster sugar
15 g/½ oz fresh yeast	

1 To make the dough with fresh yeast, sift the flour and salt into a mixing bowl and warm gently for 5–6 minutes. Rub in the lard lightly. Warm the water until tepid and blend in the yeast. Add all the water at once to the dry ingredients. Mix into a soft dough and beat well with a wooden spoon or by hand, until the dough leaves the sides of the bowl clean, adding a little extra flour if sticky, or leave this until kneading.

2 To make the dough with dried yeast, heat a cupful of the measured water until hand-hot (40°C/110°F) and add the sugar. Sprinkle the dried yeast on top, swirl it around and leave for about 10 minutes or until frothy. Add with the remaining water to the warm dry ingredients and mix to a dough as for fresh yeast.

3 Gather the dough into a ball (add more flour if sticky), turn it on to a floured board, and knead for about 10 minutes until firm, elastic and smooth. Round the dough into a ball and place in an oiled container. Leave to rise until doubled in bulk, then turn on to a board and knock back with your knuckles before shaping.

4 Mould the dough according to the type of loaf required, taking care not to work in extra flour as this will affect the colour and finish of the crust. Place the shaped dough in tins or hand mould on a baking sheet, cover with polythene and leave to rise until doubled in bulk – it will be springy to the touch when sufficiently proved. Glaze according to recipe instructions. Remove the polythene and bake the loaves in the centre of a preheated hot oven, 230°C (450°F), Gas Mark 8, for 30–40 minutes according to size. The bread is ready when the loaf begins to shrink from the sides of the tin.

5 Remove from the oven, turn out of the tin or turn upside down if hand-moulded and tap the bottom. The loaf will sound hollow when cooked. When cooked, cool by placing the loaf across the tin or on a wire rack.

Makes 1 large or 2 small loaves
Preparation time: 25 minutes, plus rising and proving
Baking time: 30–40 minutes
Oven temperature: 230°C (450°F), Gas Mark 8

Split Tin Loaf

This loaf, also called a Farmhouse Loaf, has its top slashed after proving; this makes the crust crisper and more varied in colour and texture.

- **1 recipe quantity Basic White Bread Dough (see page 10)**

1 Make the dough as for Basic White Bread, through to the end of step 4 (see page 10).
2 When you have knocked the dough back with your knuckles, shape it: flatten the ball into an oval, then fold the two curved edges over to the centre, to give straight sides. Fold in 3 lengthways into a cylinder shape. The roll should be slightly smaller than the tin so that as it expands, it domes evenly.
3 Grease and warm a 23 x 12 cm/9 x 5 inch loaf tin. Put the roll in the tin, cover with a piece of polythene and set aside to prove.
4 After the dough has proved for 10 minutes, sprinkle with water and make a deep cut lengthways down the loaf. Continue proving as for Basic White Bread.
5 Brush the loaf with salt water before baking as for Basic White Bread, allowing 40 minutes to bake.

Makes 1 large loaf
Preparation time: 25 minutes, plus rising and proving
Baking time: about 40 minutes
Oven temperature: 230°C (450°F), Gas Mark 8

VARIATION

Small Split Tin Loaves

To make two small split tin loaves, halve the risen dough before shaping it and put each half into an 18 x 10 cm/7 x 4 inch greased and warmed loaf tin. Baking time will be about 30 minutes.

Bloomer

This loaf is baked without a tin. A coating of egg wash gives it an attractive golden glaze. The Basic White Bread Dough can also be mixed with half milk and half water, if preferred.

- **1 recipe quantity Basic White Bread Dough (see page 10)**

EGG WASH:

- **1 egg**
- **1–2 tablespoons water or milk**

1 Make the dough as for Basic White Bread, through to the end of step 4 (see page 10).

2 Shape the dough into a cylinder shape, as for the Split Tin Loaf (see page 12). Put the shaped dough on a baking sheet, cover and leave for 10 minutes to prove.

3 To make the egg wash, beat the egg with the water or milk and use to brush the top of the dough. With a sharp knife, make 5 deep gashes diagonally across the top at regular intervals (it is easier if you make the centre cut first, then make two more on either side of it).

4 Continue proving for another 5–10 minutes; as the cuts open, sprinkle in some water from a pastry brush.

5 Bake immediately in a preheated oven, 230°C (450°F), Gas Mark 8 for 30 minutes. Reduce the heat to 220°C (425°F), Gas Mark 7 for a further 15 minutes, or until baked.

Makes 1 large loaf
Preparation time: 25 minutes, plus rising and proving
Baking time: about 45 minutes
Oven temperature: 230°C (450°F), Gas Mark 8; then 220°C (425°F), Gas Mark 7

VARIATION

Small Bloomers

To make 2 small bloomers, divide the risen dough in half before shaping it into cylinders. Baking time will be about 25 minutes at 230°C (450°F), Gas Mark 8, followed by about 12 minutes at 220°C (425°F), Gas Mark 7. Like the Bloomer, these small loaves can also be made with half milk and half water, if preferred.

Short Baton

The Basic White Bread Dough will make 2 or 3 of these tapered breads, which are baked on a baking sheet, like the Bloomer.

- **1 recipe quantity Basic White Bread Dough (see page 10)**

1 Make the dough as for Basic White Bread, through to the end of step 4 (see page 10).
2 Divide the risen dough into 2 or 3 pieces, forming each piece into a cylinder, as for the Bloomer (see page 13).
3 Put each cylinder on a board and gently roll to and fro with your hands, working from the centre outwards, so that the ends taper.
4 Put the shaped pieces on a baking sheet and prove for 10 minutes. Sprinkle with flour and, with a sharp knife, make a deep cut lengthways down the centre of each piece of dough. Make smaller diagonal cuts each side of the slit, if liked.
5 Continue proving for a further 10 minutes; as the cuts or gashes open, sprinkle in a little water from a pastry brush.
6 Continue to prove as for the Bloomer (see page 13). Bake in a preheated oven, 230°C (450°F), Gas Mark 8. The cooking times will vary slightly from 30 minutes, depending on the thickness of the loaves.

Makes 2 or 3 loaves
Preparation time: 25 minutes, plus rising and proving
Baking time: about 30 minutes
Oven temperature: 230°C (450°F), Gas Mark 8

Cottage Loaf

This is quite a tricky loaf to make as the dough must be stiff enough to hold its form, but not stodgy. The top-knot also tends to slide off the bottom part during baking unless carefully moulded and firmly fixed.

- 500 g/1 lb strong white flour
- 2 teaspoons salt
- 15 g/½ oz butter or lard
- 15 g/½ oz fresh yeast or 1 teaspoon dried yeast with 1 teaspoon caster sugar
- 300 ml/½ pint warm water

1 Make the dough following the recipe for Basic White Bread Dough (see page 10). When knocking back the dough after the first rise, work in a little extra flour if the dough seems slack.

2 Cut off a third of the dough and round up into one large and one small ball. Place the large ball on a floured baking sheet and flatten the top. Place the small ball beside it, leaving room for both to expand. It is best to prove the parts separately, as the weight of the top-knot tends to flatten the base. Cover and prove until nearly doubled in bulk – it is safe to under-prove slightly rather than over-prove, which would cause the loaf to spread and collapse in the oven.

3 Move the large round to the middle of the baking sheet, flatten the top again if necessary, cut a cross in the centre and brush with water. Damp the bottom of the small round and place it on top of the large round, centring it carefully.

4 Fix the two pieces firmly by pinching the dough together round the base of the top knot. Put your middle finger over your index finger, dip them together into the flour bag and then into the centre of the top-knot, pressing firmly down into the lower part of the loaf. Withdraw your fingers carefully and make sure both parts of the loaf are nicely rounded. Brush the loaf all over with salted water for a crisp crust, or dust with flour if you prefer a soft crust.

5 Bake in the centre of a preheated oven, 230°C (450°F), Gas Mark 8, for 20 minutes, then reduce the heat to 200°C (400°F), Gas Mark 6 for a further 20–25 minutes. Test by turning upside down and tapping the bottom of the loaf. If it does not sound hollow, return it to the oven for a little longer. Cool on a wire rack.

Makes 1 loaf

Preparation time: 25 minutes, plus rising and proving
Baking time: 40–45 minutes
Oven temperature: 230°C (450°F), Gas Mark 8; then 200°C (400°F), Gas Mark 6

Basic Brown Bread Dough

- 750 g/1½ lb strong wheatmeal flour
- 15 g/½ oz salt
- 15 g/½ oz lard or butter
- 15 g/½ oz fresh yeast or 2 teaspoons dried yeast with 1 teaspoon caster sugar
- 575 ml/18 fl oz warm water
- caraway seeds (optional)

1 Make the dough with fresh or dried yeast as for Basic White Bread Dough (see page 10). Knead, rise, and knock back the dough as in the Basic White Bread recipe. Shape the dough as for Split Tin Loaf (see page 12, step 2).

2 For the loaves shown follow steps 2-5 of Plain Crusty Rolls (see page 20) sprinkling with caraway seeds if liked. Bake for 20-25 minutes.

3 Grease and warm a 23 x 12 cm/9 x 5 inch loaf tin or use 2 small tins. Put the dough in the tin(s) and prove as for the Split Tin Loaf.

4 Bake the dough in a preheated oven, 230°C (450°F), Gas Mark 8, for 30–40 minutes. For a soft crust, dust with flour before baking. For a crisp crust, brush with salted water.

Makes 1 large or 2 small loaves
Preparation time: 25 minutes, plus rising and proving
Baking time: 30–40 minutes
Oven temperature: 230°C (450°F), Gas Mark 8

Brown Cob Loaf

This is a simple round loaf baked without a tin. It can also be made with all wholemeal flour or a mixture of half brown and half strong white flour.

- 1 recipe quantity Basic Brown Bread Dough (see page 16)
- cracked wheat or sesame seeds or flour, to finish

1 Divide the Basic Brown Bread Dough in half after the first rising and knocking back. Shape each piece into a round and place on a floured baking sheet. Cover with a tea towel and prove until doubled in bulk.

2 Sprinkle the dough with cracked wheat or sesame seeds, or dust with flour then bake in a preheated oven, 230°C (450°F), Gas Mark 8, for 30 minutes or until cooked.

Makes 2 loaves
Preparation time: 25 minutes, plus rising and proving
Baking time: 30 minutes
Oven temperature: 230°C (450°F), Gas Mark 8

Granary Cob Loaf

This is made in the same way as the Basic Brown Bread (see page 16) but using granary meal instead of brown flour; it is a mixture of wheat kernels and flakes, rye and wheatmeal. Granary bread has a nutty texture and some mixtures have a pleasant malty flavour.

- 750 g/1½ lb granary meal
- 2 teaspoons salt
- 15 g/½ oz fresh yeast or 2 teaspoons dried yeast with 1 teaspoon sugar
- about 575 ml/18 fl oz warm water
- 1 tablespoon vegetable oil or melted lard

1 Put the granary meal and salt into a warm bowl – it is too coarse to put through a flour sieve, so just aerate it with the fingers. Blend the yeast with 300 ml/½ pint warm water, adding the sugar if using dried yeast. Leave to froth.

2 Add the oil or fat to the remaining water, and mix with the yeast liquid. Stir into the flour and mix into a soft dough, adding a little more warm water if necessary. Do not skimp on the liquid when using coarse meals or the bread will be hard.

3 Beat well with a wooden spoon, turn on to a floured board and knead for about 10 minutes until firm and elastic. Round up the dough into a ball and put in an oiled bag or a container and leave to prove until doubled in bulk. Knock back the dough.

4 Shape and bake as for Split Tin Loaves (see page 12) or Brown Cob

Loaf (see page 17). There should be enough dough left over to make a Crown Loaf (page 19) or some Crusty Rolls (see page 20).

Makes 2 loaves or 1 loaf and some rolls

Preparation time: 25 minutes, plus rising and proving
Baking time: 30–40 minutes
Oven temperature: 230°C (450°F), Gas Mark 8

Crown Loaf

This recipe uses the dough for the Granary Cob Loaf on page 18, weighed after the dough has been proved and knocked back. It is baked in a cake tin and can be broken into portions for serving.

- 625 g/1¼ lb Granary Bread Dough, weighed when proved and knocked back (see page 18)
- milk or Egg Wash, for brushing (optional)
- poppy or sesame seeds, for sprinkling

1 Grease a 20 cm/8 inch cake tin.
2 Divide the dough into 10 equal portions, about 50 g/2 oz each. Flour your hands and roll each portion of dough into a ball between the palms of your hands.
3 Arrange 7 balls round the inside edge of the tin and fit the remaining 3 into the centre. Cover the loaf and prove for 30–35 minutes, until risen (see page 18).
4 Dust the loaf with flour for a soft crust. For a crisp crust, brush with milk, or Egg Wash (see page 13), and sprinkle with poppy or sesame seeds.
5 Bake in a preheated oven, 200°C (400°F), Gas Mark 6 for 30–35 minutes. Allow the loaf to shrink away from the sides of the tin before turning it out on to a wire rack.

Makes 1 loaf

Preparation time: 25–30 minutes, plus rising and proving
Baking time: 30–35 minutes
Oven temperature: 200°C (400°F), Gas Mark 6

Plain Crusty Rolls

These can be made with Basic White Bread Dough or Basic Brown Bread Dough. The recipe will make up to 24 rolls, depending on size, so you may find it more convenient to freeze half of the unrisen dough.

• 1 recipe quantity Basic White Bread Dough (see page 10) or 1 recipe quantity Basic Brown Bread Dough (see page 16)

1 Make the dough, according to the chosen recipe, to the first rising stage.
2 Knock back the dough after the first rising and weigh out 50 g/2 oz portions for small, round dinner rolls.
3 Roll each piece of dough into a ball between the floured palms of your hands. Press each one down on a pastry board, then release. Put the rolls on a lightly greased baking sheet, cover with polythene and leave to rise. When ready, the dough will spring back when pressed with a finger.
4 Remove the polythene and lightly brush the tops of the rolls with lightly salted water.
5 Bake in the centre of a preheated hot oven, 230°C (450°F), Gas Mark 8, for 20 minutes, or until they sound hollow when tapped. Remove from the baking sheet and cool on a wire rack.

Makes about 24
Preparation time: 25 minutes, plus rising and proving
Baking time: 20 minutes
Oven temperature: 230°C (450°F), Gas Mark 8

VARIATIONS

Knots

Weigh out the dough into 65–75 g/ 2½–3 oz portions. Roll each portion of dough into a thin sausage shape and twist into a knot. Prove, glaze and bake as for the round rolls in the main recipe. Be careful not to over-prove the dough or it will spread and lose shape in the oven.

Small Cottage Loaves

Weigh out the dough into 75 g/3 oz portions. Divide each portion into two-third and one-third pieces. Roll each piece into a ball between the floured palms of your hands. Dampen the top of the larger ball and place the smaller one on top. Push your floured forefinger or the handle of a small wooden spoon through the centre to secure the two pieces together. Prove, glaze and bake as for the round rolls in the main recipe.

Soft Wholemeal Rolls

Soft rolls are normally made with milk, or at least half milk and half water, in order to produce a soft texture. To get a soft crust, dust with flour just before baking, instead of glazing with salted water.

- **250 g/8 oz wholemeal flour**
- **1 teaspoon salt**
- **25 g/1 oz margarine or lard**
- **15 g/½ oz fresh yeast or 1½ teaspoons dried yeast with 1 teaspoon sugar**
- **about 150 ml/¼ pint warm milk**

1 Sift the flour with the salt into a mixing bowl and warm. Rub in the fat. Blend the fresh yeast with the warm milk and leave for 10 minutes to froth. If using dried yeast, dissolve the sugar in the warm milk, sprinkle in the dried yeast and leave for 15–20 minutes until frothy.

2 Pour the yeast liquid into the flour, and mix, adding a little more milk if necessary. Beat until the dough leaves the sides of the bowl clean, turn on to a floured board and knead for 10 minutes.

3 Put the dough into an oiled polythene bag and leave to rise until doubled in bulk. Knock back the dough, make a fat sausage shape and cut across into 8 equal-sized pieces. Shape into rounds or ovals. Press down firmly with the heel of your hand and release.

4 Place on a floured baking sheet, leaving space between them for expansion. Cover and prove for 15 minutes or until doubled in size.

5 Dust with flour and bake in the centre of a preheated oven, 230°C (450°F), Gas Mark 8, for 15–20 minutes. When cooked, remove to a wire rack and cover with a tea towel.

Makes 8 rolls

Preparation time: 25 minutes, plus dissolving the yeast, rising and proving
Baking time: 15–20 minutes
Oven temperature: 230°C (450°F), Gas Mark 8

Quick White Bread

The making of yeast dough can be speeded up by eliminating one rising period by adding ascorbic acid, as in this recipe, and/or increasing the amount of yeast and sugar. It enables you to make and bake one large or two small loaves in about 1¾ hours. Although satisfactory with fresh yeast, this method is not recommended for dried, which takes longer to rise and tends to give the bread too strong a yeasty flavour. Ascorbic acid is readily available in chemist shops in tablet form of 25 mg or 50 mg.

- 750 g/1½ lb strong white flour
- 15 g/½ oz salt
- 1 teaspoon sugar
- 15 g/½ oz lard
- 25 g/1 oz fresh yeast
- 450 ml/¾ pint warm water
- 25 mg ascorbic acid tablet

1 Grease 1 large or 2 small loaf tins.
2 Sift the flour and salt into a mixing bowl and leave in a warm place. Mix in the sugar and rub in the fat. Blend the yeast into the warm water, then add the ascorbic acid tablet and dissolve it. Add to the dry ingredients all at once and beat with a wooden spoon into a stiff dough, adding extra flour if necessary. When the dough leaves the sides of the bowl clean, turn on to a floured board. Knead thoroughly for 10 minutes.
3 If using an electric mixer and dough hooks, pour the yeast liquid into the mixer bowl and add the mixed dry ingredients. Mix for 1 minute on speed 1, then raise to speed 2 and knead for a further 3 minutes. Remove the dough from the mixer bowl, shape into a ball and put into an oiled polythene bag. Leave to rest for 5 minutes.
4 Stretch the dough to fit the tin or tins, fold in 3 and fit into tins. Place in a lightly oiled polythene bag. Leave for 45–50 minutes at room temperature to rise to the top of the tin. When ready, the dough will spring back when pressed.
5 Remove the polythene and bake in the centre of a preheated oven, 230°C (450°F), Gas Mark 8, for 30–35 minutes until well risen and golden brown. When it is cooked, the loaf will shrink slightly from the tin. Turn out the loaf, test by tapping the bottom, and cool across the tin or on a wire rack.

Makes 1 large or 2 small loaves, or 18 rolls

Preparation time: 25 minutes plus rising and proving
Baking time: 30–35 minutes
Oven temperature: 230°C (450°F), Gas Mark 8

Quick Brown Bread

In this one-rise bread, fresh or dried yeast may be used with the quantity slightly increased and a little extra sugar added to the mixture.

- 500 g/1 lb wholemeal flour or 250 g/8 oz wholemeal and 250 g/8 oz strong white flour
- 2 teaspoons salt
- 1 teaspoon caster sugar (optional)
- 25 g/1 oz lard or butter
- 15 g/½ oz fresh yeast or 2 teaspoons dried yeast with 1 teaspoon caster sugar
- about 350 ml/12 fl oz warm water

1 Sift the flour and salt into a mixing bowl with the sugar, if using, and rub in the fat. Prepare the yeast liquid. If using fresh yeast, blend it with a cupful of the warm water, then add it to the flour, salt and fat all at once with the remaining warm water. If using dried yeast, dissolve it in a cup of hot water (44°C/110°F) and sweeten with the sugar. Leave in a warm place for 15 minutes until frothy, then add to the dry ingredients with the remaining warm water. Beat with a wooden spoon into a fairly soft dough, adding more water if necessary.

2 Turn on to a floured board and knead well for 10 minutes. Stretch the dough to fit 1 large tin or divide in half to fit 2 small tins. Fold in three or roll up and put into the warmed and greased tins. Put in an oiled polythene bag and leave to rise in a warm place until it reaches the top edge of the tin.

3 Brush with slightly salted water and bake in the centre of a preheated oven, 230°C (450°F), Gas Mark 8, for 15 minutes. Reduce the temperature to 200°C (400°F), Gas Mark 6, and cook for a further 30–40 minutes, according to size. When cooked, the loaf will shrink slightly from the tin.

4 Turn out and tap the base to see if it sounds hollow. Remove from the oven and cool.

Makes 1 large or 2 small loaves
Preparation time: 25 minutes, plus proving
Baking time: 45–55 minutes
Oven temperature: 230°C (450°F), Gas Mark 8; then 200°C (400°F), Gas Mark 6

Muffins and Scones

Crumpets

125 g/4 oz strong white flour

125 g/4 oz plain flour

2 teaspoons salt

5 g/¼ oz fresh yeast

1 teaspoon sugar

300 ml/½ pint warm milk and water

1 tablespoon vegetable oil

½ teaspoon bicarbonate of soda

150 ml/¼ pint warm water

1 Sift the flours and salt into a warm bowl. Cream the yeast with the sugar. Add the warmed milk and water, then the oil. Stir into the flour to make a batter and beat vigorously until smooth and elastic. Cover the bowl, put in a warm place and leave until the mixture rises and the surface is full of bubbles (about 1½ hours). Break it down by beating with a wooden spoon.

2 Dissolve the bicarbonate of soda in the warm water and stir into the batter. Cover and leave in a warm place to prove for about 30 minutes.

3 To cook the crumpets, heat and grease the griddle lightly. Grease five or six 8–9 cm/3–3½ inch crumpet rings or scone cutters and put them on the griddle to heat. Cook as many crumpets as possible at a time as the batter will not remain bubbly for long.

4 Put 1 cm/½ inch of batter into each ring. Cook gently for 7–10 minutes, or until the surface sets and is full of tiny bubbles. Using an oven glove for protection, lift off the ring and if the base of the crumpet is pale gold, flip it over and cook for another 3 minutes until the other side is just coloured.

5 If the crumpet batter is set but sticks slightly in the ring, push it out gently with the back of a wooden spoon. Wipe, grease and heat the rings for each batch of crumpets.

Makes 12–14

Preparation time: 20 minutes, plus rising and proving

Cooking time: 10–13 minutes per batch

Tea Cakes

- 500 g/1 lb plain flour
- 1 teaspoon salt
- 2 teaspoons sugar
- 100 g/4 oz currants
- 25 g/1 oz fresh yeast
- 300 ml/½ pint warm milk
- melted butter, for brushing

1 Sift the flour and salt into a mixing bowl and add the sugar and currants.
2 Cream the yeast with a little extra sugar and some of the warm milk. Pour the yeast mixture into a well in the centre of the flour and leave in a warm place for 10 minutes.
3 Add the remaining milk to the yeast mixture, mix to a light dough and knead well. Cover the bowl with polythene or a clean tea towel and put in a warm place to rise for about 1–1½ hours until doubled in size.
4 Knead the dough again, then divide it into 8 pieces and roll and shape them into round tea cakes. Prick each one with a fork. Put the tea cakes on a greased baking sheet, cover with a cloth and stand in a warm place to prove for 30 minutes.
4 Transfer the tea cakes to a preheated oven, 220°C (425°F), Gas Mark 7, and bake for 10–12 minutes. Remove the tea cakes from the oven, brush them with melted butter, then return to the oven for a further 10 minutes.
5 To serve, split each tea cake in half, toast lightly and spread with butter.

Makes 8
Preparation time: 25 minutes, plus rising and proving
Cooking time: 20–22 minutes
Oven temperature: 220°C (425°F), Gas Mark 7

Muffins

These are cooked on the griddle like crumpets, but are made with a yeast dough instead of a batter. They should be served very hot, generously buttered, in a hot dish with a cover – the Victorians produced very attractive silver or decorative china muffin dishes.

- 500 g/1 lb strong white flour
- 1 tablespoon salt
- 15 g/½ oz fresh yeast or 1½ teaspoons dried yeast
- 1 teaspoon sugar
- 250 ml/8 fl oz warm milk and water
- 50 g/2 oz butter, melted

1 Sift the flour and salt into a bowl and leave in a warm place. Dissolve the yeast and sugar in 150 ml/¼ pint of the warm milk and water. Leave to froth, then mix in the fat. Stir all the liquid into the warm flour and beat well until smooth and elastic. Cover and prove in a warm place for 50 minutes or until doubled in bulk.

2 Turn on to a well floured board and knead, working in a little more flour if necessary to make the dough easy to shape. Round up the dough, roll into a thick sausage shape and divide into 8–10 portions, about 1–2 cm/½–¾ inch thick.

3 Shape each one into a round with straight sides. Put on to a greased baking sheet. Cover and put in a warm place to prove for 30–40 minutes, or until springy to the touch. Leave room for expansion and be careful not to

over-prove as the muffins will lose their shape.

4 Warm the griddle gently and grease lightly with a small piece of lard on a fork. Lift the muffins carefully on to the griddle and cook over very moderate heat for 8–10 minutes until they are pale gold underneath. Turn them over and cook the other side. Wrap the muffins in a cloth and keep them warm in a low oven if you are cooking in batches.

5 To serve, insert a knife in the side, then with fingers, pull the top and bottom apart and insert thin slices of butter. If reheating from cold, toast the top and bottom, then pull apart and add the butter.

Makes 8–10
Preparation time: 20–25 minutes, plus rising and proving
Cooking time: 12–14 minutes per batch

Hot Apple Muffins

These American muffins are quite different from the traditional English variety, being raised with baking powder. They are quite delicious split and buttered for breakfast and very quick and easy to make. They are served hot and can be reheated on a baking sheet covered loosely with foil in a hot oven at 220°C (425°F), Gas Mark 7 for 5–6 minutes.

- 250 g/8 oz plain flour
- 1 teaspoon salt
- 1 tablespoon baking powder
- 50 g/2 oz caster sugar
- 2 eggs, beaten
- 150 ml/¼ pint milk
- 50 g/2 oz butter, melted
- 250 g/8 oz cooking or dessert apples, peeled, cored and chopped fairly small

1 Grease 1 x twenty four 5 cm/2 inch bun or muffin tins.

2 Sift the flour, salt, baking powder and sugar into a mixing bowl. In a small bowl beat the eggs with the milk and mix in the melted butter. Stir the liquid quickly into the flour mixture. Speed is essential once the liquid is added to the baking powder, so do not beat the mixture or bother about any lumps. Fold in the chopped apples.

3 Spoon the mixture into the greased bun tins so they are one-third full. Bake in a preheated oven, 220°C (425°F), Gas Mark 7, for 15–20 minutes or until the muffins are well risen and golden brown. Turn out of the tins and serve hot.

Makes 24

Preparation time: 10 minutes
Baking time: 15–20 minutes
Oven temperature: 220°C (425°F),
Gas Mark 7

Oven Scones

These scones are very quick and easy to make. Serve them for tea fresh from the oven: you will have time to boil the kettle to make a pot of tea while the scones are baking.

- 250 g/8 oz plain white or wheatmeal flour
- ½ teaspoon salt
- 4 teaspoons baking powder
- 25–50 g/1–2 oz butter or margarine
- 150 ml/¼ pint milk
- a little water
- milk or flour, to finish

1 Sift the flour, salt and baking powder into a mixing bowl. Cut the fat into the flour and rub in with the fingertips to a breadcrumb consistency. Make a well in the centre, pour in the milk and mix to a soft spongy dough, adding a little water if necessary.

2 Turn the dough out on to a well-floured board, and knead quickly and lightly. Roll out the dough with a floured rolling pin or flatten with floured hands until it is 1.5 cm/¾ inch thick. Cut into rounds using a 6 cm/ 2½ inch floured pastry cutter or a tumbler. Place the scones on a warmed baking sheet.

3 Shape the remaining dough into a ball, flatten into a circle, cut out more rounds and place on the baking sheet. Brush the scones with milk for a glazed finish or rub them with flour for a soft crust. Bake near the top of a preheated oven, 230°C (450°F), Gas Mark 8, for 7–10 minutes, until well risen and golden on top.

4 To serve, split the scones and spread with butter, cream and jam.

Makes about 12

Preparation time: 12 minutes
Baking time: 7–10 minutes
Oven temperature: 230°C (450°F), Gas Mark 8

Cheese Scones

These savoury scones are excellent with high tea or supper. Serve them with salads and egg dishes, or with hot soup in place of bread rolls.

- 250 g/8 oz plain flour
- ½ teaspoon salt
- 1 teaspoon dry mustard
- 4 teaspoons baking powder
- 50 g/2 oz butter or margarine
- 75–100 g/3–4 oz mature Cheddar cheese, grated
- 1 egg, beaten
- 150 ml/¼ pint milk or water

TO FINISH:

- milk
- grated cheese

1 Sift the flour, salt, mustard and baking powder into a mixing bowl. Cut the fat into the flour and rub in to a breadcrumb consistency. Mix in the grated cheese. Beat the egg with half of the liquid and stir into the dry ingredients. Work into a soft dough adding more liquid as necessary.

2 Turn on to a well-floured board and roll out lightly until 1.5 cm/¾ inch thick. Cut out rounds with a 6.5 cm/2½ inch cutter. Work the remaining dough into a round and cut more rounds. Place all the rounds on a warmed baking sheet. Brush with milk and sprinkle with grated cheese.

3 Bake in a preheated oven, 220°C (425°F), Gas Mark 7, for 10–15 minutes until well risen and golden.

Cool on a wire rack. Serve with butter, cream cheese or a salad filling.

Makes about 12
Preparation time: 12 minutes
Baking time: 10–15 minutes
Oven temperature: 220°C (425°F), Gas Mark 7

Girdle Scones

Scones can be cooked very successfully on a girdle or griddle instead of in the oven. The method is economical with fuel. The traditional griddle is thick cast iron with a hoop handle which folds down for storage. It should be heated slowly and evenly. Gas or electric burners tend to concentrate the heat in the centre of the griddle so the scones must be watched and moved around so they brown evenly. The heat should be kept moderate or the scones will brown outside before they are cooked through. Test the heat of a griddle by sprinkling it with flour which should take a few minutes to turn biscuit colour. A well-seasoned griddle which has frequent use will not need greasing for scone doughs, except for drop scones and similar batter mixtures.

- **1 recipe quantity Oven Scone Dough (see page 29)**

1 Follow the recipe for Oven Scones (see page 29), making a soft but not sticky dough. Divide it in two and knead lightly until smooth. Roll out each half into a round 1 cm/½ inch thick and cut across into four or six equal triangles.
2 Cook on the heated griddle for about 5 minutes until nicely browned underneath. Turn and cook the other side until the scones are golden and cooked through completely.
3 Wrap the scones in a cloth if they are to be served hot, or cool on a wire rack.
4 Girdle scones left overnight can be split, toasted, and buttered and served hot the following day.

Makes 8–12
Preparation time: 12 minutes
Cooking time: about 10 minutes per batch

VARIATION

Fruited Girdle Scones

Add 50 g/2 oz sultanas and 25 g/1 oz caster sugar to the basic Oven Scone recipe. Shape and bake as for Girdle Scones. Cool on a wire tray and serve with butter or clotted cream.

Drop Scones

These are sometimes called Scotch pancakes as they are made with a batter, not a dough. There are a variety of recipes but the following is excellent for tea-time, being quick and easy to make.

- 125 g/4 oz self-raising flour
- 2 tablespoons caster sugar
- 1 egg, beaten
- about 150 ml/¼ pint milk

1 Sift the flour into a mixing bowl and mix in the sugar. Make a well in the centre and drop in the egg. Stir in the milk gradually and mix to a creamy batter. The thicker the batter, the thicker the pancake will be.
2 Heat a griddle and grease it lightly. Using a large spoon, drop the batter off the point in round 'puddles' on to the griddle, leaving space for spreading. Cook over a moderate heat until the top surface is covered with bubbles, and when the underneath is golden, turn over with a palette knife and cook the other side.
3 When golden, lift off the griddle and wrap in a cloth. Serve as soon as possible with butter, honey or preserves.
4 If any scones are left until the next day, they can be crisped under the grill before serving.

Makes 18
Preparation time: 10 minutes
Cooking time: 6–7 minutes per batch

Honey and Cream Scones

These delicious scones can be cooked on the griddle, as well as in the oven.

• 175 g/6 oz wholemeal flour
• 175 g/6 oz plain flour
• 2 teaspoons bicarbonate of soda
• 1 teaspoon cream of tartar
• 25 g/1 oz butter or margarine
• 150 ml/¼ pint soured cream
• 125 g/4 oz clear honey
• 1 egg
• milk, for glazing

1 Sift the two flours, soda and cream of tartar into a mixing bowl. Cut the fat into the flour and rub in with the fingertips until it has a breadcrumb consistency. Mix the soured cream and honey together until the honey is dissolved. Beat in the egg.
2 Make a well in the flour, pour in the liquid and mix to a soft dough.
3 Turn on to a floured board and knead in a little extra flour, if necessary. Roll out to 1 cm/½ inch thick and cut into rounds with a 5 cm/2 inch cutter. Work up the trimmings into a round and cut into 4 triangles. Place on a warmed floured baking sheet and brush the scones with milk.
4 Bake near the top of a preheated oven, 230°C (450°F), Gas Mark 8, for about 10 minutes.
5 Serve hot, split and spread with butter and honey, or cold, spread with butter or clotted cream.

Makes about 12

Preparation time: 12–15 minutes
Baking time: about 10 minutes
Oven temperature: 230°C (450°F), Gas Mark 8

Family Cakes and Sponges

Chocolate Cake

This is a very easy cake to make. Its deliciously rich texture makes it good for a dessert, too. Try serving it with whipped cream or vanilla ice cream.

200 g/7 oz plain flour	150 ml/¼ pint milk
1 teaspoon bicarbonate of soda	CHOCOLATE ICING:
1 teaspoon baking powder	175 g/6 oz plain chocolate
2 tablespoons cocoa powder	2 tablespoons single cream
150 g/5 oz soft brown sugar	TO DECORATE:
2 tablespoons golden syrup	75 g/3 oz walnut halves
2 eggs	icing sugar
150 ml/¼ pint oil	

1 Line and grease a 23 cm/9 inch cake tin.

2 Sift the dry ingredients into a mixing bowl and make a well in the centre. Add the golden syrup, eggs, oil and milk and beat thoroughly until smooth.

3 Pour into the prepared tin and bake in a preheated oven 160°C (325°F), Gas Mark 3, for 45–50 minutes.

4 Leave the cake in the tin for a few minutes then turn on to a wire rack to cool.

5 To make the icing, put the chocolate and cream into a small pan and heat gently until melted. Cool slightly, then pour over the cake. Dredge the walnuts with icing sugar and arrange in the centre of the cake.

Makes one 23 cm/9 inch cake

Preparation time: 15 minutes

Baking time: 45–50 minutes

Oven temperature: 160°C (325°F), Gas Mark 3

Ginger Cake

This is really a double ginger cake, for it contains both ground ginger and chopped preserved ginger.

- 175 g/6 oz butter or margarine
- 175 g/6 oz caster sugar
- 3 eggs
- 250 g/8 oz self-raising flour
- ½ teaspoon ground ginger
- 75 g/3 oz preserved ginger, chopped
- 2 tablespoons ginger syrup

GINGER ICING:

- 175 g/6 oz icing sugar, sifted
- 2 tablespoons ginger syrup
- preserved ginger strips, to decorate

1 Line and grease an 18 cm/7 inch cake tin.

2 Cream the fat and sugar together until light and fluffy. Add the eggs one at a time, adding a tablespoon of flour with the last two. Sift and fold in the remaining flour and the ground ginger, then fold in the preserved ginger and syrup. Turn into the prepared tin.

3 Bake in a preheated oven, 180°C (350°F), Gas Mark 4, for 1–1¼ hours. Turn out on to a wire rack to cool.

4 To make the ginger icing, beat the icing sugar and syrup together until smooth. Pour over the cake and leave until set. Decorate with ginger strips.

Makes one 18 cm/7 inch cake

Preparation time: 20 minutes
Baking time: 1–1¼ hours
Oven temperature: 180°C (350°F), Gas Mark 4

Victoria Sandwich Cake

Turn this light sponge cake into a special treat by sandwiching the layers with whipped cream as well as jam.

- 125 g/4 oz butter or margarine
- 125 g/4 oz caster sugar
- 2 eggs
- 125 g/4 oz self-raising flour, sifted
- 1 tablespoon hot water

TO FINISH:

- 150 ml/¼ pint double cream, lightly whipped
- 3 tablespoons jam
- caster sugar

1 Line and grease two 18 cm/7 inch sandwich tins.
2 Cream the fat and sugar together until light and fluffy. Beat in the eggs, one at a time, adding a tablespoon of the flour with the second egg. Fold in the rest of the flour, then the water.
3 Divide the mixture between the prepared tins and bake in a preheated oven, 180°C (350°F), Gas Mark 4, for 20–25 minutes, until the cakes are golden and spring back when lightly pressed. Turn on to a wire rack to cool.
4 Sandwich the cakes together with the cream and jam and sprinkle the top with caster sugar.

Makes one 18 cm/7 inch cake
Preparation time: 15 minutes
Baking time: 20–25 minutes
Oven temperature: 180°C (350°F), Gas Mark 4

Angel Cake

You will need a special angel cake tin to make this recipe, but you will not have to grease it, as this helps the mixture hold its shape in the tin.

- 25 g/1 oz plain flour
- 25 g/1 oz cornflour
- 150 g/5 oz caster sugar
- 5 large egg whites
- 1 teaspoon vanilla essence
- 150 ml/¼ pint double cream, lightly whipped
- 125 g/4 oz fresh raspberries
- 50 g/2 oz redcurrants
- icing sugar, for sprinkling

1 Sift the flours and 25 g/1 oz of the caster sugar together 3 or 4 times.

2 Whisk the egg whites until stiff, add the remaining caster sugar, a tablespoon at a time, and continue whisking until very thick.

3 Carefully fold in the sifted mixture with the vanilla essence and turn into a 20 cm/8 inch angel cake tin. Smooth the surface and bake in a preheated moderate oven, 180°C (350°F), Gas Mark 4, for 35–40 minutes, until the cake springs back when lightly pressed.

4 Turn the cake upside down on a wire rack and leave in the tin until cold, when the cake will fall easily from the tin. Fill the well with the cream, raspberries and redcurrants and serve sprinkled with icing sugar.

Makes one 20 cm/8 inch cake
Preparation time: 20 minutes
Baking time: 35–40 minutes
Oven temperature: 180°C (350°F), Gas Mark 4

Banana Cake

- 125 g/4 oz butter or margarine
- 125 g/4 oz caster sugar
- 2 eggs
- 125 g/4 oz self-raising flour, sifted
- 2 bananas, mashed
- icing sugar, to dust

FILLING:

- 50 g/2 oz ground almonds
- 50 g/2 oz icing sugar, sifted
- 1 small banana, mashed
- ½ teaspoon lemon juice

1 Line and grease two 18 cm/7 inch sandwich tins.

2 Cream the fat and sugar together until light and fluffy. Add the eggs, one at a time, adding a tablespoon of flour with the second egg. Fold in the remaining flour with the bananas.

3 Divide the mixture between the prepared sandwich tins. Bake in a preheated moderate oven, 180°C (350°F), Gas Mark 4, for 20–25 minutes until the cakes spring back when lightly pressed. Turn out the cakes on to a wire rack to cool.

4 To make the filling, mix the ground almonds with the icing sugar, then add the banana and lemon juice and mix to a smooth paste. Sandwich the cakes together with the filling and dust with icing sugar.

Makes one 18 cm/7 inch cake

Preparation time: 15 minutes
Baking time: 20–25 minutes
Oven temperature: 180°C (350°F), Gas Mark 4

Genoese Sponge

- 50 g/2 oz butter
- 4 eggs
- 125 g/4 oz caster sugar
- 125 g/4 oz plain flour, sifted

TO FINISH:
- 150 ml/5 fl oz double cream
- 2 tablespoons lemon curd
- icing sugar

1 Line and grease a 23 cm/9 inch moule à manqué tin.
2 Warm the butter gently until just soft – do not allow it to become oily. Whisk the eggs and sugar in a mixing bowl over a pan of hot water until thick enough to leave a trail. Remove from the heat and whisk until cool. (Hot water is unnecessary if you are using an electric beater.)
3 Fold in the flour; when it is almost incorporated, fold in the butter as rapidly as possible, being careful not to knock out the air. Turn at once into the prepared tin. Bake in a preheated oven, 190°C (375°F), Gas Mark 5, for 30–35 minutes, until the cake springs back when lightly pressed. Leave in the tin for 1 minute then turn on to a wire rack to cool.
4 Whip the cream until stiff then whisk in the lemon curd. Split the cake in half and sandwich together with the lemon cream. Sprinkle with icing sugar.

Makes one 23 cm/9 inch cake
Preparation time: 15–20 minutes
Baking time: 30–35 minutes
Oven temperature: 190°C (375°F), Gas Mark 5

Whisked Sponge

The ideal whisk for this sponge is a wire balloon whisk, because it incorporates so much air, although a hand-held electric beater is quicker. A moule à manqué tin is a deep sandwich tin with slightly sloping sides.

- **4 eggs**
- **140 g/4½ oz caster sugar**
- **125 g/4 oz plain flour, sifted**

TO FINISH:

- **150 ml/¼ pint double cream, whipped**
- **selection of fruit**
- **icing sugar**

1 Line, grease and flour a 23 cm/9 inch moule à manqué tin.

2 Whisk the eggs and sugar in a mixing bowl over a pan of boiling water until thick enough to leave a trail. (Hot water is unnecessary if you are using an electric beater.)

3 Fold in the flour, then pour the mixture into the prepared tin. Bake in a preheated oven, 190°C (375°F), Gas Mark 5, for 35–40 minutes, until the cake springs back when lightly pressed.

4 Turn on to a wire rack to cool. Split the cake in half, then fill with the cream and and three-quarters of the fruit. Arrange the remaining fruit on top and sprinkle with icing sugar.

Makes one 23 cm/9 inch cake

Preparation time: 15 minutes
Baking time: 35–40 minutes
Oven temperature: 190°C (375°F), Gas Mark 5

Swiss Roll

- 3 eggs
- 75 g/3 oz caster sugar
- 75 g/3 oz plain flour, sifted
- 1 tablespoon hot water
- 3 tablespoons warmed jam
- caster sugar, for dredging

1 Line and grease an 18 x 28 cm/7 x 11 inch Swiss roll tin.

2 Whisk the eggs and sugar in a mixing bowl over a pan of hot water until thick enough to leave a trail. (Hot water is unnecessary if you are using an electric beater.) Fold in the flour and the water, then turn into the prepared Swiss roll tin.

3 Bake in a preheated oven, 200°C (400°F), Gas Mark 6, for 8–10 minutes, until the cake springs back when lightly pressed.

4 Turn on to sugared greaseproof paper, peel off the lining paper and trim the edges. Cut a slit two-thirds of the way through the short edge nearest you, then spread lightly with the jam and roll up quickly. Hold in position for a few minutes, then transfer to a wire rack to cool. Dredge with caster sugar before serving.

Makes 1 Swiss roll

Preparation time: 15 minutes
Baking time: 8–10 minutes
Oven temperature: 200°C (400°F), Gas Mark 6

Cherry Cake

- 175 g/6 oz butter or margarine
- 175 g/6 oz caster sugar
- 3 eggs
- 300 g/10 oz self-raising flour, sifted
- 250 g/8 oz glacé cherries, halved
- 50 g/2 oz ground almonds
- about 5 tablespoons milk

1 Line and grease a deep 18 cm/7 inch cake tin.

2 Cream the fat and sugar together until light and fluffy. Beat in the eggs one at a time, adding a tablespoon of flour with the last two.

3 Carefully fold in the remaining flour, then fold in the cherries, ground almonds and enough milk to give a dropping consistency.

4 Put the mixture into the prepared tin and bake in a preheated oven, 160°C (325°F), Gas Mark 3, for 1½–2 hours.

5 Leave the cherry cake in the tin for 5 minutes, then turn on to a wire rack to cool.

Makes one 18 cm/7 inch cake

Preparation time: 20 minutes
Baking time: 1½–2 hours
Oven temperature: 160°C (325°F), Gas Mark 3

Madeira Cake

This Madeira cake may be frozen for up to 6 months. Thaw completely, still in its wrapping or lining paper and foil, at room temperature before use, perhaps in the Coco the Clown Cake (see pages 84–85).

- 175 g/6 oz butter
- 175 g/6 oz caster sugar
- 175 g/6 oz self-raising flour
- 75 g/3 oz plain flour
- 3 eggs
- grated rind and juice of 1 lemon

1 Grease and single-line an 18 cm/ 7 inch round cake tin.

2 Cream the butter with the sugar until light, fluffy and very pale.

3 Sift the self-raising and plain flours together. Beat the eggs into the creamed mixture, one at a time, following each addition with a spoonful of sifted flour.

4 Fold in the remaining flour, followed by the grated lemon rind and juice.

5 Bake in a preheated oven, 160°C (325°F), Gas Mark 3, for 1¼ hours, or until well-risen, firm to the touch and golden brown.

6 Cool in the tin for 5–10 minutes, then turn on to a wire rack and leave until cold. Do not peel off the lining paper but wrap the cake as it is in foil or store in an airtight container until required.

Makes one 18 cm/7 inch round cake or one 1 kg/2 lb loaf cake
Preparation time: 20 minutes
Baking time: 1¼ hours
Oven temperature: 160°C (325°F), Gas Mark 3

Dundee Cake

This classic fruit cake makes a good Christmas cake for those who do not care for marzipan or royal icing. Make the cake's top look more festive by including some halved glacé cherries and strips of glacéd peel among the almonds.

- 175 g/6 oz plain flour
- 1 teaspoon ground mixed spice
- 125 g/4 oz butter or margarine
- 125 g/4 oz soft brown sugar
- grated rind of ½ orange or lemon
- 3 eggs
- 125 g/4 oz sultanas
- 125 g/4 oz currants
- 125 g/4 oz raisins
- 50 g/2 oz glacé cherries, quartered
- 25 g/1 oz chopped mixed peel
- 40 g/1½ oz split blanched almonds to decorate

1 Grease a deep 15 cm/6 inch cake tin and line the base and sides with a double layer of greased greaseproof paper. Tie a thick band of brown paper around the outside of the tin and stand it on a pad of brown paper placed on a baking sheet.

2 Sift the flour and spice together. Cream the fat, sugar and orange rind together until light and fluffy. Beat in the eggs one at a time, adding a tablespoon of flour with the last two. Fold in the remaining flour and the fruit until thoroughly mixed.

3 Put the mixture into the prepared tin, smooth the top and decorate with the almonds. Bake in a preheated oven, 160°C (325°F), Gas Mark 3, for 1 hour, then lower the temperature to 150°C (300°F), Gas Mark 2 and bake for a further 2–2½ hours, or until a skewer inserted into the centre comes out clean.

4 Leave in the tin for 5 minutes then turn on to a wire rack to cool.

Makes one 15 cm/6 inch cake

Preparation time: 25 minutes
Baking time: 3–3½ hours
Oven temperature: 160°C (325°F), Gas Mark 3; then 150°C (300°F), Gas Mark 2

Everyday Fruit Cake

As well as being a good tea-time cake, this is excellent for school lunch boxes.

- 250 g/8 oz self-raising flour
- ½ teaspoon ground mixed spice
- ½ teaspoon ground cinnamon
- 125 g/4 oz butter or margarine
- 125 g/4 oz soft brown sugar
- 125 g/4 oz currants
- 50 g/2 oz glacé cherries, quartered
- 1 large egg
- 5 tablespoons milk

1 Line and grease a deep 15 cm/6 inch cake tin.

2 Sift the self-raising flour, mixed spice and cinnamon into a mixing bowl, add the fat and rub in with the fingertips until the mixture resembles breadcrumbs. Stir in the sugar, currants and glacé cherries. Whisk the egg and milk together, add to the mixture and beat thoroughly.

3 Put the mixture into the prepared tin and bake in a preheated oven, 180°C (350°F), Gas Mark 4, for 1¼–1½ hours. Leave the cake in the tin for a few minutes, then turn it out on to a wire rack to cool.

Makes one 15 cm/6 inch cake
Preparation time: 20 minutes
Baking time: 1¼–1½ hours
Oven temperature:180°C (350°F), Gas Mark 4

Sticky Gingerbread

If you prefer, replace the ground ginger in this recipe with finely chopped fresh root ginger.

- 250 g/8 oz plain flour
- 3 teaspoons ground ginger
- 1 teaspoon ground mixed spice
- 1 teaspoon bicarbonate of soda
- 125 g/4 oz butter or margarine
- 75 g/3 oz black treacle
- 125 g/4 oz golden syrup
- 50 g/2 oz soft brown sugar
- 150 ml/¼ pint milk
- 2 eggs, beaten
- 25 g/1 oz shredded almonds

1 Line and grease an 18 cm/7 inch square cake tin.

2 Sift the flour, spices and soda into a mixing bowl. Put the fat, treacle, syrup and sugar into a pan and heat gently. Cool slightly then add to the dry ingredients with the milk and eggs and mix thoroughly.

3 Pour the mixture into the prepared tin and sprinkle with the almonds.

4 Bake in a preheated oven, 160°C (325°F), Gas Mark 3, for 1½–2 hours, or until a skewer inserted into the centre comes out clean.

5 Leave in the tin for 15 minutes, then turn on to a wire rack. Store in an airtight tin for some days before eating.

Makes one 18 cm/7 inch cake

Preparation time: 15 minutes, plus cooling
Baking time: 1½–2 hours
Oven temperature: 160°C (325°F), Gas Mark 3

Cookies and Pâtisserie

Mocha Slices

25 g/1 oz butter	125 g/4 oz icing sugar, sifted
2 eggs	125 g/4 oz unsalted butter
50 g/2 oz caster sugar	1 tablespoon coffee essence
50 g/2 oz plain flour, sifted	COFFEE ICING:
apricot glaze (see page 89)	250 g/8 oz icing sugar, sifted
COFFEE BUTTER CREAM:	2 teaspoons coffee essence
2 egg whites	1½ tablespoons water

1 Line and grease an 18 cm/7 inch square shallow tin.

2 Prepare the sponge as for Genoese Sponge (see page 40). Turn the mixture into the prepared tin and bake in a preheated oven, 190°C (375°F), Gas Mark 5, for 25–30 minutes. Turn on to a wire rack to cool, then split in half.

3 To make the coffee butter cream, whisk the egg whites and sugar together over a pan of simmering water until the mixture holds its shape. Cool slightly. Cream the butter until soft, then add the meringue mixture a little at a time. Stir in the coffee essence.

4 Use some of the butter cream to sandwich the cake together, then cut the cake into ten fingers.

5 Brush the apricot glaze over the fingers to coat completely. Leave to set.

6 To make the icing, combine the icing sugar, coffee essence and water, then spread over the fingers and leave to set.

7 Pipe the remaining butter cream in a zig-zag along the middle of each slice.

Makes 10

Preparation time: 30 minutes

Baking time: 25–30 minutes

Oven temperature: 190°C (375°F), Gas Mark 5

Langues de Chat

These delicate biscuits are ideal for serving with desserts such as mousses, creams and ice creams.

- 50 g/2 oz butter
- 50 g/2 oz caster sugar
- 2 egg whites
- 50 g/2 oz plain flour, sifted
- a few drops of vanilla essence

1 Cream the butter and sugar together until light and fluffy. Whisk the egg whites lightly and gradually beat into the creamed mixture. Carefully fold in the flour and vanilla essence.
2 Place the mixture in a piping bag fitted with a 2 cm/⅜ inch plain nozzle and pipe 7 cm /3 inch lengths on a greased and floured baking sheet.
3 Bake in a preheated oven, 200°C (400°F), Gas Mark 6, for 10 minutes; the biscuits should be pale golden but darker around the edges. Transfer to a wire rack to cool.

Makes 20–24
Preparation time: 15 minutes
Baking time: 10 minutes
Oven temperature: 200°C (400°F), Gas Mark 6

Walnut Fudge Biscuits

- 185 g/6½ oz plain flour
- ½ teaspoon salt
- ½ teaspoon bicarbonate of soda
- 125 g/4 oz butter or margarine, softened
- 125 g/4 oz soft brown sugar
- 50 g/2 oz granulated sugar
- 1 egg
- ½ teaspoon vanilla essence
- 125 g/4 oz chopped walnuts

CHOCOLATE ICING:

- 50 g/2 oz butter or margarine
- 25 g/1 oz plain chocolate
- 2 tablespoons milk
- 200 g/7 oz icing sugar
- ½ teaspoon vanilla essence

1 Sift the flour, salt and bicarbonate of soda into a bowl. Set aside.

2 Put the butter or margarine and brown and granulated sugars into a bowl and cream until light and fluffy. Stir in the egg and beat well. Add the vanilla essence and mix well.

3 Gradually add the flour mixture until just blended. Stir in the walnuts.

4 Drop rounded teaspoonfuls of the mixture slightly apart on to ungreased baking sheets. With your finger or a teaspoon, make a hollow in the centre of each one.

5 Put the biscuits in a preheated oven, 190°C (375°F), Gas Mark 5, and bake for 5 minutes. Press the hollows down again, then continue baking for 4–5 minutes until the biscuits are golden.

6 While the biscuits are baking, make the icing. Put the butter or margarine and chocolate in the top of a double boiler over simmering water. Heat, stirring occasionally, until the chocolate melts. Blend in the milk. Remove from heat; mix in the icing sugar and vanilla until smooth.

7 Transfer the biscuits to wire racks to cool. Fill the centres with icing, dividing it evenly.

Makes about 48 biscuits
Preparation time: 25 minutes
Baking time: 9–10 minutes
Oven temperature: 190°C (375°F), Gas Mark 5

Japonais

- 50 g/2 oz ground almonds
- 125 g/4 oz caster sugar
- 2 egg whites

COFFEE BUTTER ICING:

- 40 g/1½ oz butter
- 75 g/3 oz icing sugar, sifted
- 1 teaspoon milk
- 1 teaspoon coffee essence

TO FINISH:

- 25 g/1 oz ground almonds, browned, to finish
- icing sugar

1 Mix together the almonds and sugar and set aside. Whisk the egg whites until stiff, then fold in the almond mixture. Spoon the mixture into a piping bag fitted with a 1 cm/½ inch plain nozzle and pipe sixteen 5 cm/ 2 inch rounds on a piece of non-stick paper placed on a baking sheet.

2 Bake in a preheated oven, 150°C (300°F), Gas Mark 2, for 30–35 minutes. Transfer to a wire rack.

3 To make the coffee butter icing, cream the fat with half of the icing sugar until soft, then add the milk, coffee essence and the remaining icing sugar. Beat well.

4 Sandwich the rounds together in pairs with some of the butter icing and spread more round the sides.

5 Press ground almonds round the side of each cake. Leave to set, then dust with icing sugar.

Makes 8

Preparation time: 15 minutes
Baking time: 30–35 minutes
Oven temperature: 150°C (300°F),
Gas Mark 2

Pecan Snaps

These little biscuits can be left flat after baking, or they can be shaped in a number of ways. To make 'curls' shape the slightly cooled biscuits over a rolling pin; for 'cigarettes', roll them round a lightly greased wooden spoon handle; and for 'tulips', drape them over a tumbler 6–7 cm/2½–3 inches in diameter, pressing the biscuit gently into a cup shape. Let the biscuits cool and set before carefully removing them from their moulds. The tulips are delicious filled with ice cream and topped with a hot butterscotch sauce.

- 50 g/2 oz butter or margarine
- 50 g/2 oz soft brown sugar
- 3 tablespoons golden syrup
- 40 g/1½ oz plain flour
- 50 g/2 oz pecan nuts, finely chopped
- 1 teaspoon vanilla essence

1 Grease and lightly flour two baking sheets.
2 Melt the butter in a medium saucepan over gentle heat. Stir in the brown sugar and the syrup. Increase the heat to high and bring the mixture to a boil, stirring constantly, until the brown sugar has dissolved.
3 Remove the pan from the heat. Stir in the flour and pecans until well combined. Blend in the vanilla.
4 Place rounded spoonfuls of the mixture on to the prepared baking sheets about 5 cm/2 inches apart. For 'curls' or 'cigarettes', drop teaspoonfuls on the baking sheets; to make 'tulips' drop tablespoonfuls on the sheets,

7 cm/3 inches apart. Using a small palette knife spread the mixture into an even circle.
5 Bake in a preheated oven, 180°C (350°F), Gas Mark 4, for 6–8 minutes for small biscuits and 8–10 minutes for large ones, or until they are browned. If the biscuits become too cool to shape, return them to the oven briefly to soften.

Makes about 30 small or 8–10 large biscuits

Preparation time: 10–12 minutes
Baking time: 6–8 minutes (small biscuits), 8–10 minutes (large biscuits)
Oven temperature: 180°C (350°F), Gas Mark 4

Cream Horns

- 225 g/7½ oz frozen puff pastry, thawed
- beaten egg, to glaze
- strawberry jam
- 175 ml/6 fl oz double cream, whipped

TO DECORATE:

- glacé cherries, halved
- angelica
- icing sugar

1 Roll out the pastry into a rectangle about 25 x 33 cm/10 x 13 inches and trim the edges. Cut into 10 strips 2.5 cm/1 inch wide.

2 Dampen one long edge of each strip with water and wind round 10 cornet moulds, starting at the point and overlapping the dampened edge. Gently press the edges together. Place on a dampened baking sheet, cover and chill for 15 minutes.

3 Brush with egg and bake in a preheated oven, 220°C (425°F), Gas Mark 7, for 15–20 minutes until golden brown. Leave for 5 minutes before carefully removing the moulds. Cool on a wire rack.

4 Spoon a little jam into each horn then pipe in the cream. Decorate with pieces of cherry and angelica and sprinkle with icing sugar.

Makes 10

Preparation time: 20 minutes, plus chilling
Baking time: 15–20 minutes
Oven temperature: 220°C (425°F), Gas Mark 7

Almond Butter Cookies

- **175 g/6 oz plain flour**
- **½ teaspoon baking powder**
- **125 g/4 oz butter or margarine, softened**
- **75 g/3 oz sugar**
- **½ teaspoon vanilla essence**
- **2 tablespoons water**

PRALINE:

- **125 g/4 oz sugar**
- **25 g/1 oz almonds**

1 First make the praline. Put the sugar and almonds in a small, heavy-based pan over medium-high heat and stir occasionally until the sugar dissolves and turns a pale amber colour.

2 Pour out the caramel mixture on to a greased and lined baking sheet, to make a layer 5 mm/¼ inch thick and spread with an oiled palette knife. Set aside until cold.

3 Break the praline into pieces and put them into a polythene bag. Crush the pieces coarsely with a rolling pin.

4 To make the cookies, sift the flour and baking powder into a bowl, then set aside.

5 Put the butter and sugar into a large bowl and cream until light and fluffy. Add the vanilla essence and mix well.

6 Add the flour mixture alternately with the water, mixing until smooth after each addition. Stir the crushed praline into the mixture.

7 Drop rounded teaspoonfuls, 5 cm/ 2 inches apart, on to well-greased baking sheets. Bake in a preheated oven, 160°C (325°F), Gas Mark 3, for

14–16 minutes or until the edges are lightly browned. Leave the cookies on the baking sheets for 2 minutes, then carefully transfer to wire racks to cool completely.

Makes about 36

Preparation time: 20 minutes, including cooling the praline
Baking time: 14–16 minutes
Oven temperature: 160°C (325°F), Gas Mark 3

Walnut Barquettes

PATE SUCREE:

- 125 g/4 oz plain flour
- 50 g/2 oz butter, softened
- 50 g/2 oz caster sugar
- 2 egg yolks
- few drops vanilla essence

WALNUT FILLING:

- 50 g/2 oz butter
- 50 g/2 oz caster sugar
- 1 egg, beaten
- 25 g/1 oz plain flour, sifted
- 50 g/2 oz walnuts, ground

ICING:

- 125 g/4 oz icing sugar, sifted
- 1 egg white

1 To make the pâte sucrée, sift the flour on to a large board, make a well in the centre and put the butter, sugar, egg yolks and vanilla essence into the well. Using the fingertips of one hand, work these ingredients together until well blended, then draw in the flour. Knead lightly until smooth and chill for 1 hour.

2 Roll out the pastry thinly and use to line 14 barquette moulds. Prick and chill for 20 minutes.

3 To make the walnut filling, cream together the butter and sugar until light and fluffy, then add the egg and flour and beat well. Fold in the walnuts.

4 Spoon the mixture into a piping bag fitted with a plain nozzle and pipe into the chilled pastry cases.

5 To make the icing, mix the icing sugar with the egg white until smooth. Spoon into a piping bag fitted with a writing nozzle and pipe a criss-cross

pattern over each of the cakes.

6 Bake in a preheated oven, 190°C (375°F), Gas Mark 5, for 20 minutes. Leave in the moulds for 5 minutes, then transfer to a wire rack to cool completely.

Makes 14
Preparation time: 35 minutes, plus chilling
Baking time: 20 minutes
Oven temperature: 190°C (375°F), Gas Mark 5

Mille Feuilles

- 500 g/1 lb puff pastry
- 3 tablespoons strawberry jam
- 175 ml/6 fl oz double cream, whipped
- icing sugar, for sprinkling

1 Roll out the pastry into a large thin sheet, prick all over and cut into twenty 10 x 6 cm/4 x 2½ inch pieces. Place on dampened baking sheets and chill for 15 minutes.

2 Bake in a preheated hot oven, 220°C (425°F), Gas Mark 7, for 8–10 minutes until dark golden brown. Transfer to a wire rack to cool then split each piece in half.

3 Spread strawberry jam on the cut sides of 10 of the pieces of puff pastry and top with the whipped cream. Cover with the remaining 10 pieces of puff pastry and press down firmly. Sprinkle the tops with icing sugar.

4 Holding it with an oven glove or thick cloth, carefully heat a metal skewer and score a criss-cross pattern across the tops of the mille feuilles.

Makes 20

Preparation time: 20 minutes, plus chilling
Baking time: 8–10 minutes
Oven temperature: 220°C (425°F), Gas Mark 7

Italian Candied Slices

- 300 g/10 oz plain flour
- 1½ teaspoons baking powder
- ¼ teaspoon salt
- ¼ teaspoon aniseeds, coarsely crushed
- 50 g/2 oz butter or margarine, softened
- 225 g/7½ oz granulated sugar
- 1 teaspoon vanilla essence
- 2 teaspoons grated orange rind
- 3 eggs
- 150 g/5 oz unblanched whole almonds
- 75 g/3 oz mixed candied fruit
- 50 g/2 oz glacé cherries
- 1 tablespoon coarse sugar, such as demerara, or crushed sugar cubes (optional)

1 Sift the flour, baking powder and salt into a bowl, add the aniseeds, then set aside.

2 Cream the butter and granulated sugar in a large bowl. Blend in the vanilla and orange rind. Separate 1 of the eggs and reserve the white. Add the yolk to the creamed mixture, then add the remaining 2 eggs, one at a time, beating well after each addition.

3 Gradually beat in the flour mixture until the dough is smooth and well blended. Divide the dough in half and wrap each portion in clingfilm. Cover and chill for about 1 hour until firm.

4 Meanwhile, mix together the almonds, candied fruit and glacé cherries in a bowl.

5 On a lightly floured surface, roll out 1 portion of the dough to a 30 x 20 cm/12 x 8 inch rectangle. Sprinkle with half the fruit mixture. Starting with a 30 cm/12 inch edge, roll up the rectangle like a Swiss roll. Pinch the edge and ends to seal. Place the roll, sealed side down, on a lightly greased baking sheet. Repeat with the remaining dough.

6 Beat the reserved egg white until slightly frothy then brush over each roll. Sprinkle the rolls lightly with coarse sugar, if liked.

7 Using a serrated knife cut the rolls on the diagonal into 1 cm/½ inch thick slices. Place, cut sides down, on lightly greased baking sheets and bake in a preheated oven, 180°C (350°F), Gas Mark 4, for 20 minutes until crisply toasted. Transfer to wire racks to cool completely.

Makes about 48

Preparation time: 35 minutes, plus chilling
Baking time: 20 minutes
Oven temperature: 180°C (350°F), Gas Mark 4

Fresh Lemon Slices

- 250 g/8 oz butter or margarine, softened
- 75 g/3 oz icing sugar
- 1 teaspoon vanilla essence
- 250 g/8 oz plain flour
- 4 eggs
- 175 g/6 oz granulated sugar
- grated rind of 1 lemon
- 6 tablespoons lemon juice

1 Generously grease a 30 x 23 cm/12 x 9 inch shallow baking tin.

2 Put the butter, 50 g/2 oz of the icing sugar and the vanilla essence into a bowl and cream until light and fluffy. Sift the flour and fold, a little at a time, into the creamed mixture until completely incorporated. Spread the mixture evenly in the prepared tin and bake in a preheated oven, 190°C (375°F), Gas Mark 5, for 20 minutes.

3 Meanwhile, put the eggs, granulated sugar, lemon rind and lemon juice into a bowl. Stir to blend the ingredients but do not beat. Pour the mixture over the baked pastry layer.

4 Return the tin to the oven and bake for 18–22 minutes until the topping is set and lightly browned.

5 Remove the tin from the oven and sift the remaining icing sugar over the warm cake to cover it generously. Cut the cake into slices. Remove from the tin when cool.

Makes 36

Preparation time: 15 minutes
Baking time: 38–42 minutes
Oven temperature: 190°C (375°F), Gas Mark 5

Double Orange Slices

- 25 g/1 oz plain flour
- ½ teaspoon baking powder
- 2 eggs
- 250 g/8 oz soft brown sugar
- 1 teaspoon vanilla essence
- 1 tablespoon grated orange rind
- 125 g/4 oz shelled walnuts, chopped
- 140 g/4½ oz desiccated coconut

ORANGE PASTRY:

- 125 g/4 oz butter or margarine, softened
- 125 g/4 oz granulated sugar
- 1 teaspoon grated orange rind
- 125 g/4 oz plain flour

ORANGE GLAZE:

- 175 g/6 oz icing sugar
- 1 teaspoon grated orange rind
- 1½ tablespoons orange juice

1 Lightly grease a 30 x 23 cm /12 x 9 inch shallow baking tin.

2 To make the orange pastry, cream the butter, sugar, and orange rind until light and fluffy. Gradually work in the flour until mixture is like fine breadcrumbs. Press the pastry firmly and evenly into the prepared tin.

3 Bake in a preheated oven, 190°C (375°F), Gas Mark 5, for 10 minutes. Remove from the oven. Reduce the heat to 180°C (350°F), Gas Mark 4.

4 Sift the flour and baking powder into a bowl. Cream the eggs and brown sugar in a second bowl until well mixed. Blend in the vanilla and orange rind. Gradually beat in the flour mixture until well combined. Stir in the walnuts and coconut. Spread the mixture over the partially baked pastry and bake for 20–25 minutes or until well browned and set in the centre. Remove the tin to a rack.

5 To make the orange glaze, mix the sugar and orange rind, then stir in the juice until the icing is smooth. Drizzle over the pastry while still warm.

6 Leave the cake to stand until the glaze is set then cut into slices in the tin. Remove from the tin when cold.

Makes 36

Preparation time: 25–30 minutes
Baking time: 30–35 minutes
Oven temperature: 190°C (375°F),
Gas Mark 5; then 180°C (350°F), Gas
Mark 4

Frangipane Tartlets

SHORTCRUST PASTRY:

• 25 g/1 oz butter

• 25 g/1 oz lard

• 125 g/4 oz plain flour, sifted

• water, to mix

FILLING:

• 50 g/2 oz butter

• 50 g/2 oz caster sugar

• 1 egg, beaten

• 1 tablespoon flour

• 50 g/2 oz ground almonds

• 2 drops of almond essence

• 25 g/1 oz flaked almonds

• 2 tablespoons apricot glaze (see page 89)

1 To make the pastry, rub the fat into the flour until the mixture resembles breadcrumbs. Stir in enough water to make a firm dough. Knead lightly, cover and chill for 30 minutes.

2 Roll out the pastry thinly, cut into ten 7 cm/3 inch circles and use to line 10 deep patty tins. Chill again for 15 minutes.

3 Cream together the butter and sugar until light and fluffy, add the egg, then beat in the flour. Mix in the ground almonds and almond essence.

4 Spoon into a piping bag fitted with a 1 cm/½ inch plain nozzle and two-thirds fill the pastry cases. Sprinkle the tartlets with flaked almonds. Bake in a preheated oven, 200°C (400°F), Gas Mark 6, for 20 minutes. Transfer to a wire rack then brush with the apricot glaze and leave to set.

Makes 10

Preparation time: 20 minutes, plus chilling

Baking time: 20 minutes

Oven temperature: 200°C (400°F), Gas Mark 6

Aurora Tartlets

These tartlets earned their unusual name because the filling of peaches coated in redcurrant glaze is crimson, like the sun at dawn. Poached fresh peaches can be used when in season, instead of canned.

ALMOND PASTRY:

- 175 g/6 oz plain flour
- pinch of salt
- 125 g/4 oz ground almonds
- 75 g/3 oz caster sugar
- 125 g/4 oz butter, softened
- 1 egg, beaten
- 1 teaspoon grated lemon rind

FILLING:

- 12 tablespoons Pastry Cream (see page 90)
- 12 canned peach halves, sliced
- Redcurrant Glaze (see page 89)

1 To make the pastry, sift the flour and salt on to a board. Mix in the ground almonds and sugar. Make a well in the centre and add the butter, egg and grated lemon rind. Work together with the fingers of one hand, gradually drawing in the dry ingredients and using a knife in the other hand to gather them together. Knead into a smooth dough. Put into a polythene bag and leave in a cool place to relax for at least 1 hour before rolling out.
2 Roll out the cooled pastry very thinly and use to line 12 shallow 5 cm/2 inch tartlet tins. Put on a baking sheet, prick well and line each one with a small piece of foil.
3 Bake in a preheated oven, 200°C (400°F), Gas Mark 6, for 10 minutes.

Remove the foil and return the pastry to the oven for a further 5 minutes until crisp and golden. Lift out of the tin and cool on a wire rack.
4 Put a spoonful of pastry cream in each tartlet and arrange a few peach slices on top. Warm the redcurrant glaze and spoon or brush evenly over the peaches. Serve cold.

Makes 12
Preparation time: 30 minutes, plus cooling the pastry
Baking time: 15 minutes
Oven temperature: 200°C (400°F), Gas Mark 6

Custard Tarts

A rich egg custard flavoured with vanilla and sprinkled with spice makes a delightfully smooth filling for these crisp pastry tarts.

SWEET SHORTCRUST PASTRY:
- 250 g/8 oz plain flour
- pinch of salt
- 50 g/2 oz butter
- 50 g/2 oz lard or vegetable shortening
- 25 g/1 oz caster sugar
- 1 egg yolk
- a little water

CUSTARD:
- 450 ml/¾ pint milk
- 2 eggs
- 2–3 teaspoons sugar
- ¼ teaspoon vanilla essence
- grated nutmeg, to finish

1 To make the pastry, sift the flour and salt into a bowl. Rub the fat into the flour until the mixture resembles breadcrumbs, then mix in the sugar. Beat the egg yolk with 2 tablespoons water and stir in to bind to a fairly firm dough, adding a little more water as necessary. Knead lightly until smooth but do not overwork. Cover and leave to rest in the refrigerator for at least 30 minutes before rolling out.
2 Grease 8 small, deep 5 cm/2 inch muffin tins.
3 Roll out the cooked pastry thinly. Cut out 7 cm/3 inch rounds and use to line the muffin tins. Bake blind in a preheated oven, 200°C (400°F), Gas Mark 6, for 12–15 minutes until set but not brown, then remove from the oven. Lower the heat to 160°C (325°F), Gas Mark 3.

4 To make the custard, warm the milk over a low heat and while it is heating beat together the eggs and sugar. Stir the warm milk into the beaten eggs and flavour with vanilla essence. Strain the custard into the partially baked cases.
5 Sprinkle the tops with grated nutmeg and return the tarts to the centre of the oven for 15–20 minutes until the custard is set. Serve cold.

Makes 8
Preparation time: 30 minutes, plus cooling the pastry
Baking time: 27–35 minutes
Oven temperature: 200°C (400°F), Gas Mark 6; then 160°C (325°F), Gas Mark 3

Bittersweet Biscuits

- 200 g/7 oz plain flour
- ¼ teaspoon salt
- ¼ teaspoon bicarbonate of soda
- ¼ teaspoon baking powder
- 1 tablespoon instant coffee granules
- 125 g/4 oz butter or margarine, softened
- 50 g/2 oz vegetable cooking fat
- 125 g/4 oz granulated sugar
- 125 g/4 oz soft brown sugar
- 1½ teaspoons vanilla essence
- 1 egg yolk
- about 3 tablespoons granulated sugar
- 50 g/2 oz chocolate coffee beans

1 Sift the flour, salt, bicarbonate of soda, baking powder and instant coffee into a bowl, then set aside.
2 Put the butter or margarine and cooking fat into a large bowl and cream until light and fluffy. Add the sugars and beat until well blended. Beat in the vanilla, then the egg yolk. Gradually add the flour mixture, beating until just well combined.
3 Shape the mixture into 2.5 cm/ 1 inch balls and place them about 5 cm/2 inches apart on ungreased baking sheets. Dip a tumbler in granulated sugar and use it to flatten each biscuit to a 5 mm/¼ inch thickness. Press a chocolate coffee bean in the centre of each one.
4 Bake the biscuits in a preheated oven, 190°C (375°F), Gas Mark 5, for 10–12 minutes, until they are golden brown and firm to the touch. Leave to cool on the baking sheets for 1–2 minutes, then transfer to wire racks to cool completely.

Makes about 36
Preparation time: 20 minutes
Baking time: 10–12 minutes
Oven temperature: 190°C (375°F), Gas Mark 5

French Honey and Fruit Biscuits

These are one of the many varieties of petit fours and are a marvellous way to use trimmings of almond pastry. Any mixture of glacé or crystallized fruit can be used. Apricot jam or ginger marmalade can be used to sandwich the biscuits together instead of honey if you prefer.

- **75 g/3 oz glacé or crystallized fruit, finely chopped**
- **1 tablespoon rum**
- **125 g/4 oz Almond Pastry (see page 62)**
- **3–4 tablespoons thick honey**
- **icing sugar, for dusting**

1 Soak the fruit in the rum for at least 30 minutes.
2 Roll out the pastry, sprinkle with the fruit, fold it up and knead lightly until the fruit is well mixed into the dough. Roll out fairly thinly and cut into 5 cm/2 inch rounds.
3 Place the rounds on a greased baking sheet and bake in a preheated oven, 190°C (375°F), Gas Mark 5, for 10–12 minutes until set and golden. Cool on a wire rack and sandwich together in pairs with honey. To serve dust lightly with sieved icing sugar.

Makes about 9
Preparation time: 15 minutes, plus soaking
Baking time: 10–12 minutes
Oven temperature: 190°C (375°F), Gas Mark 5

Butterscotch Nut Brownies

These American cookies are made by the melting method and taste like delicious baked fudge. They keep well in an airtight tin or plastic container. Blanched almonds and cashew nuts can be used instead of hazelnuts and walnuts.

- 125 g/4 oz butter
- 500 g/1 lb soft brown sugar
- 2 eggs, beaten
- ½ teaspoon vanilla essence
- 125 g/4 oz plain flour
- 2 teaspoons baking powder
- 1 teaspoon salt
- 250 g/8 oz hazelnuts and walnuts, coarsely chopped

1 Grease and line the base of a shallow 20 cm/8 inch square tin.
2 Melt the butter in a saucepan over gentle heat, then mix in the sugar and stir until dissolved. Cool slightly and beat in the eggs and vanilla essence.
3 Sift the flour with the baking powder and salt and mix in thoroughly. Stir in the hazelnuts and walnuts and pour into the prepared tin.
4 Bake in a preheated oven, 190°C (375°F), Gas Mark 5, for about 30 minutes or until set, but not hard. Cut into 16 squares while still hot, then allow to cool in the tin. When cold, lift out carefully.

Makes 16
Preparation time: 15 minutes
Baking time: about 30 minutes
Oven temperature: 190°C (375°F), Gas Mark 5

VARIATION

Coconut Brownies

Follow the recipe for Butterscotch Nut Brownies and substitute 50 g/2 oz grated or desiccated coconut for the chopped nuts.

Vanilla and Sesame Wafers

- **50 g/2 oz sesame seeds**
- **65 g/2½ oz plain flour**
- **¼ teaspoon baking powder**
- **⅛ teaspoon salt**
- **125 g/4 oz butter or margarine, softened**
- **125 g/4 oz soft brown sugar**
- **1 egg**
- **1 teaspoon vanilla essence**

1 Spread the sesame seeds in a shallow tin and bake in a preheated oven, 160°C (325°F), Gas Mark 3, stirring occasionally, for 6–8 minutes, or until lightly toasted. Set aside.
2 Sift the flour, baking powder and salt into a bowl, then set aside.
3 Cream the butter and brown sugar in a bowl until light and fluffy. Beat in the egg. Add the vanilla and mix well.
4 Gradually add the flour mixture until just blended. Add the roasted sesame seeds and stir until well combined.
5 Place rounded teaspoonfuls, about 5 cm/2 inches apart, on greased baking sheets. Bake in the oven for 9–10 minutes or until the biscuits are lightly browned. They are very fragile when they first come out of the oven so leave them on the baking sheets to cool for about 1 minute, then carefully transfer to wire racks to cool completely.

Makes about 48

Preparation time: 20 minutes
Baking time: 15–18 minutes
Oven temperature: 160°C (325°F), Gas Mark 3

Butterscotch Shortbread

- 125 g/4 oz butter or margarine, softened
- 50 g/2 oz soft dark brown sugar
- ½ teaspoon vanilla essence
- 150 g/5 oz plain flour
- 25 g/1 oz ground almonds

1 Lightly grease a 23 cm/9 inch square baking tin and dust it with flour.
2 Cream the butter and brown sugar until light and fluffy. Blend in the vanilla essence. Gradually fold in the flour and then the ground almonds until they are completely absorbed and the mixture is stiff.
3 Pat evenly and firmly into a smooth layer in the prepared tin. Bake in a preheated oven, 160°C (325°F), Gas Mark 3, for 30–35 minutes or until the top feels firm when touched gently and the edges pull away from the sides of the tin.
4 Leave the shortbread to cool in the tin on a wire rack for about 10 minutes. Cut into 16 squares; then cut each one in half diagonally to make 2 triangles. Remove from the tin when cool.

Makes 32
Preparation time: 15 minutes
Baking time: 30–35 minutes
Oven temperature: 160°C (325°F), Gas Mark 3

Chocolate Cinnamon Crunchies

- 250 g/8 oz plain flour
- 2 teaspoons bicarbonate of soda
- 1 teaspoon ground cinnamon
- ¼ teaspoon salt
- 125 g/4 oz butter or margarine, softened
- 50 g/2 oz vegetable shortening
- 275 g/9 oz sugar
- ½ teaspoon vanilla essence
- 1 egg
- 3 tablespoons golden syrup
- 50 g/2 oz plain chocolate, melted and cooled

1 Sift the flour, bicarbonate of soda, cinnamon and salt into a bowl, then set aside.

2 In a large bowl, beat together the butter and shortening. Add 225 g/ 7½ oz of the sugar and beat until fluffy. Add the vanilla, then the egg, beating well. Blend in the syrup and chocolate. Gradually work in the dry ingredients, beating until just well combined.

3 Spread the remaining sugar in a shallow tin. Shape the dough into balls about 3½ cm/1½ inches in diameter. Place the balls, 6–8 at a time in the tin and roll in the sugar to coat them lightly all over. Place the balls about 5 cm/2 inches apart on ungreased baking sheets.

4 Bake in a preheated oven, 180°C (350°F), Gas Mark 4, for about 15 minutes or until the cookies feel firm when touched lightly. Leave the cookies on the baking sheets for about 2 minutes, then transfer to wire racks to cool completely.

Makes 36
Preparation time: 20 minutes
Baking time: about 15 minutes
Oven temperature: 180°C (350°F), Gas Mark 4

Festive Cakes

Simnel Cake

175 g/6 oz butter or margarine

175 g/6 oz caster sugar

3 large eggs, lightly beaten

250 g/8 oz plain flour

1 teaspoon ground cinnamon

1 teaspoon ground nutmeg

375 g/12 oz currants

125 g/4 oz sultanas

75 g/3 oz chopped mixed peel

1–2 tablespoons milk

500 g/1 lb Marzipan (see page 86)

3–4 tablespoons apricot jam

1 egg, beaten, for glazing

1 Line an 18 cm/7 inch round cake tin. Cream the butter and sugar and beat in the eggs a tablespoon at a time, beating well between each addition. Sift the flour with the spices and fold it in, then the fruit. Mix to a soft dropping consistency with a little milk. Put half the mixture into the prepared tin and level it off.

2 Divide the marzipan into 3 and roll out one-third into a round slightly smaller than the tin. Pinch the edges to prevent the paste cracking. Lay the round on the cake mixture then cover with the remaining cake mixture and level it off. Tie a band of brown paper round the outside of the tin, to come 5 cm/2 inches above it to protect the top of the cake during baking. Put it in a preheated oven with the top of the cake in the centre of the oven and bake at 160°C (325°F), Gas Mark 3 for 1 hour. Reduce the heat to 150°C (300°F), Gas Mark 2 for a further 2 hours or until the cake is firm to the touch.

3 Allow to cool in the tin before turning out on to a wire rack to cool. Leave on the lining paper, wrap the cake in foil and store for at least 2 weeks.

4 When required, unwrap the cake. Heat the jam and sieve if lumpy. Roll out one reserved piece of marzipan into a round for the cake top. Brush the apricot glaze over the cake top and press on the marzipan. Pinch the edge of the marzipan into flutes.

5 Flatten the remaining marzipan and divide into 11 equal parts. Roll each one into a small ball. Brush the top and sides of the marzipan on the cake with beaten egg. Press on the balls round the edge of the cake. Glaze with beaten egg. Brown under a hot grill. Cool the cake.

Makes one 18 cm/7 inch cake

Preparation time: 25 minutes, plus storing time

Baking time: 3 hours

Oven temperature: 160°C (325°F), Gas Mark 3; then 150°C (300°F), Gas Mark 2

Hot Cross Buns

These spiced yeast buns are traditionally served hot on Good Friday. Nowadays they can be made well in advance, closely wrapped and frozen and, when required, defrosted and heated in a hot oven. Alternatively you can make the dough on the previous day, put it into an oiled polythene bag and chill overnight. Next day, when it has doubled in bulk, knock it back and make the buns.

- 500 g/1 lb strong white flour
- 150 ml/¼ pint milk
- 4 tablespoons water
- 25 g/1 oz fresh yeast or 15 g/½ oz dried yeast
- 1 teaspoon caster sugar
- 1 teaspoon salt
- ½ teaspoon mixed spice
- ½ teaspoon ground cinnamon
- ½ teaspoon grated nutmeg
- 50 g/2 oz caster sugar
- 50 g/2 oz butter or margarine
- 1 egg, beaten
- 125 g/4 oz currants
- 40 g/1½ oz chopped mixed peel
- 50 g/2 oz shortcrust pastry

GLAZE:
- 3 tablespoons caster sugar
- 4 tablespoons milk and water mixed

1 Put 125 g/4 oz of the flour into a small bowl. Warm the milk and water, then blend in the yeast and the teaspoon of sugar. Mix this into the flour and leave in a warm place to froth for about 15 minutes for fresh yeast, about 20 minutes for dried.

2 Meanwhile, sift the remaining flour, salt, mixed spice, cinnamon, nutmeg and sugar into a mixing bowl. Melt and cool the butter, but do not allow it to harden, then add it to the frothy yeast mixture with the beaten egg. Stir this into the flour and mix well with a wooden spoon. Scatter the currants and mixed peel into the mixture and mix to a fairly soft dough. Add a spoonful of water if necessary.

3 Turn the dough on to a floured board and knead well. Put into an oiled polythene bag and leave to rise for 1–1½ hours at room temperature until doubled in bulk. Turn on to a floured board and knock back the dough.

4 Divide into 12 pieces and shape into small round buns. Press down briefly on each bun with the palm of the hand, then place the buns well apart on a floured baking sheet. Cover and put in a warm place to rise for 20–30 minutes until doubled in size.

Meanwhile, roll out the pastry thinly and cut into 24 thin strips about 9 cm/3½ inches long.

5 When the buns have risen, damp the pastry strips and lay 2 strips across each bun to make a cross. Bake the buns in a preheated oven, 190°C (375°F), Gas Mark 5, for 20 minutes or until they are golden brown and firm to the touch.

6 Meanwhile, make the glaze by dissolving the sugar in the milk and water mixture over low heat. When the buns are ready brush them twice with the glaze. Serve the buns hot, split and buttered.

Makes 12
Preparation time: 30 minutes, plus rising
Baking time: about 20 minutes
Oven temperature: 190°C (375°F), Gas Mark 5

Amaretti

These macaroons are made in various sizes and in Italy are used in many ways – the small ones for petit fours and decoration, and larger ones crushed and incorporated into ices and dessert creams.

- 125 g/4 oz ground almonds
- 15 g/½ oz ground rice or rice flour
- 250 g/8 oz caster sugar
- ¼ teaspoon ratafia essence
- 2 egg whites
- 2 sheets of rice paper
- 12 blanched almonds, split
- 1 egg white, beaten, for glazing

1 Mix together the ground almonds, ground rice or flour and caster sugar. Add the ratafia essence to the unbeaten egg whites and mix into the dry ingredients. Cream to a smooth paste (a blender will save time).

2 Put the mixture into a piping bag with a plain 1 cm/½ inch nozzle. Rule the rice paper into 5 cm/2 inch squares. Pipe the mixture into the centre of each square, making biscuits 2.5 cm/1 inch in diameter, and flatten slightly. Press a split almond into the centre of each macaroon. Brush lightly with beaten egg white.

3 Bake in a preheated moderate oven, 180°C (350°F), Gas Mark 4, for about 20 minutes or until golden brown. Cool on a wire rack and cut off the rice paper round each macaroon. Store in an airtight tin.

Makes 24

Preparation time: 15 minutes
Baking time: about 20 minutes
Oven temperature: 180°C (350°F), Gas Mark 4

Christmas Cake

This cake can be made just a week or two before Christmas as it does not need so long to mature as the dark spicy variety. The fresh citrus flavour and lighter texture appeal to young children as well as adults.

- 250 g/8 oz butter
- 250 g/8 oz caster sugar
- grated rind and juice of 1 orange
- grated rind and juice of 1 lemon
- 4 eggs, beaten
- 275 g/9 oz plain flour
- 175 g/6 oz sultanas
- 125 g/4 oz glacé cherries, chopped
- 75 g/3 oz glacé pineapple, chopped
- 50 g/2 oz candied orange and lemon peel, chopped
- 25 g/1 oz candied citron peel or angelica, chopped
- 125 g/4 oz crystallized ginger, chopped
- 50 g/2 oz walnuts, chopped
- 50 g/2 oz blanched almonds, shredded
- 3 tablespoons sherry
- 1 recipe quantity Marzipan (see page 86)
- 1 recipe quantity Royal Icing (see page 88)

1 Line a 20 cm/8 inch round cake tin.
2 Cream the butter and sugar with the orange and lemon rind until light and fluffy. Beat in the eggs, a tablespoonful at a time, beating well between each addition. Add a spoonful of the flour at any sign of curdling.
3 Fold in the flour alternately with the fruit, candied peel, ginger and nuts. When thoroughly mixed, stir in the orange and lemon juice and sherry. Turn into the prepared cake tin and make a deep hollow in the centre. Tie a band of brown paper round the outside of the tin and 5 cm/2 inches above it to protect the top of the cake.
4 Place in a preheated oven so that the top of the cake is in the centre and bake at 180°C (350°F), Gas Mark 4 for 20 minutes. When the cake starts to brown, put a sheet of greaseproof paper over the top (resting on the collar) to prevent it over-browning. Reduce the heat to 150°C (300°F), Gas Mark 2 for a further 2¾ hours. A skewer inserted in the centre will come out clean when the cake is cooked. Remove the cake from the tin, leaving on the lining paper, and cool on a wire rack. When cold, put it in an airtight tin until coating with marzipan.
5 To cover the cake with marzipan, shape the marzipan into a fat sausage and divide into 3 equal portions. Sprinkle the pastry board with icing sugar and roll out 1 portion of the marzipan into a round to fit on top of the cake, using the base of the cake tin as a guide. Brush the top of the cake with beaten egg white, press on the marzipan round and mould the edges to fit neatly. Roll the sugared rolling pin across it to flatten it evenly.
6 Measure round the cake with a piece of string and cut the string in half. Roll the remaining 2 portions of marzipan out on the sugared board to the same length as the string, with the width matching the height of the cake. Brush the sides of the cake with beaten egg white. Press one strip of marzipan round half the cake, then repeat with the other half. Knead all the joins neatly together. Stand a jam jar against the cake and roll it round the cake, pressing on the paste firmly and evenly, smoothing out the joins and sharpening the angle round the top edge.
7 Leave the cake, covered with a clean cloth, in a warm, dry place overnight for the marzipan to dry out and firm up before coating with royal icing.
8 To ice the cake, place it on a large upturned plate. Reserving a little for decoration, put a mound of royal icing in the centre of the top. With a palette knife, spread it out evenly to the edges, covering the top completely. Now coat the sides, making sure the icing meets round the top edge of the cake. Clean the knife with hot water, shake off any drops and, holding it horizontally, at an angle, draw it across the top of the cake, ending at the edge with an upwards movement and leaving the icing smooth. Clean the knife and, with the rounded end, draw up the icing into peaks all round the sides of the cake and round the edge of the top to give a rough snow effect.

Makes one 20 cm/8 inch cake
Preparation time: 35 minutes, plus marzipaning and icing the cake
Baking time: 3 hours
Oven temperature: 180°C (350°F), Gas Mark 4; then 150°C (300°F), Gas Mark 2

Panettone

This sweet yeast cake is a traditional part of Christmas fare in Italy, but it is served with coffee and for breakfast throughout the year in many regions. Panettone keeps well in an airtight container and can be reheated whole.

- about 375 g/12 oz plain flour
- ¼ teaspoon salt
- 15 g/½ oz fresh yeast or 1½ teaspoons dried yeast
- 50 g/2 oz caster sugar
- 4 tablespoons warm water
- 3 eggs or 6 egg yolks
- ¼ teaspoon vanilla essence
- 2 teaspoons finely grated lemon rind
- 125 g/4 oz butter, softened
- 75 g/3 oz sultanas
- 40 g/1½ oz candied citron peel, chopped
- 25 g/1 oz butter, melted

1 Grease and line a 500 g/1 lb or an 18 cm/7 inch round cake tin.

2 Sift about 250 g/8 oz of the flour and the salt into a bowl and put to warm. Dissolve the yeast in the warm water with a teaspoon of the sugar and leave in a warm place to froth.

3 Mix the remaining sugar into the flour. Beat the eggs with the vanilla and lemon rind. Stir into the flour, a third at a time, and mix into a soft dough which can be gathered into a ball. Gradually beat in the butter. Add a little more flour, working the dough with your hands into a manageable ball. Turn it on to a floured board and knead for about 10 minutes until smooth and silky, then put it into a warm bowl, cover and leave for 45–50 minutes, or until doubled in bulk.

4 Knock back the dough and knead in the sultanas and peel. Shape the dough into a ball, put into the prepared tin and cut a cross in the top. Leave in a warm place for about 15–20 minutes or until doubled in bulk.

5 Brush the top of the panettone with melted butter and bake in the centre of a preheated oven, 200°C (400°F), Gas Mark 6, for 10 minutes. Brush again with melted butter and reduce the heat to 180°C (350°F), Gas Mark 4 for a further 40 minutes, or until the top is crisp and golden and a skewer inserted comes out clean. Cool on a wire rack. Serve cut into thick wedges.

Serves 6–8
Preparation time: 30 minutes, plus rising and proving the dough
Baking time: about 50 minutes
Oven temperature: 200°C (400°F), Gas Mark 6; then 180°C (350°F), Gas Mark 4

Devil's Food Chocolate Cake

This is a rich dark cake with fluffy, crisp white frosting, decorated with melted chocolate. You will need a sugar thermometer to make its traditional American frosting.

- 125 g/4 oz plain chocolate, broken into pieces
- 150 g/5 oz butter
- 125 g/4 oz dark brown sugar
- 1 tablespoon golden syrup
- 200 g/7 oz plain flour
- 15 g/1 oz cocoa powder, more for dusting
- 1 teaspoon bicarbonate of soda
- 2 eggs, beaten
- 125 ml/4 fl oz milk

AMERICAN FROSTING:
- 250 g/8 oz granulated sugar
- 125 ml/4 fl oz water
- 1 egg white
- a few drops of vanilla essence or 1 teaspoon coffee essence or 1 teaspoon lemon juice

1 Baseline and grease a deep straight-sided 20 cm/8 inch cake tin. Heat the chocolate in a saucepan with the butter, sugar and syrup until they have just melted.

2 Sift the flour, cocoa and bicarbonate of soda into a bowl. Make a well in the centre and stir in the cooled melted ingredients. Stir in the eggs and beat well, then mix in the milk. Pour the mixture into the prepared tin.

3 Bake in a preheated oven, 180°C (350°F), Gas Mark 4, for 30 minutes or until set. Allow the cake to cool in the tin before turning out on to a wire rack to cool.

4 While the cake is cooling make the American frosting. Put the sugar and water in a heavy-based pan over low heat and dissolve the sugar without stirring. Bring to the boil and continue boiling, without stirring, until a sugar thermometer registers 114°C (240°F). Just before this temperature is reached, whisk the egg white in a clean, dry bowl until stiff. Remove the syrup from the heat and when the bubbles have subsided, pour the syrup in a thin stream on to the egg white, whisking continuously. When the frosting is thick and opaque, add your chosen flavouring.

5 Coat the top and sides of the cake with the American frosting, swirling it with a palette knife, working quickly before it sets.

6 When the frosting has set, lightly dust the top of the cake with a little cocoa powder.

Makes one 20 cm/8 inch cake
Preparation time: 20 minutes
Baking time: 30 minutes
Oven temperature: 180°C (350°F), Gas Mark 4

Rich Shortbread

A carved wooden shortbread mould could be used to make shortbread, but the mixture can be pressed into a fluted flan ring which will prevent it spreading and losing shape during baking. Decorated with a sprig of heather tied up with tartan ribbon, shortbread makes an attractive Christmas gift.

- 250 g/8 oz plain flour
- 125 g/4 oz rice flour or ground rice
- 125 g/4 oz caster sugar
- pinch of salt
- 250 g/8 oz unsalted butter

1 Sift the two flours (or flour and rice), sugar and salt into a mixing bowl. Soften the butter slightly, cut it up and rub it into the dry ingredients with your fingers. When the mixture starts to bind, gather it together with one hand into a ball. Knead it on a lightly floured board until it is a soft, smooth and pliable dough.

2 Put a 20 cm/8 inch flan ring on a greased baking sheet and put in the dough, pressing it out evenly with your knuckles to fit the ring. With the back of a knife, mark the shortbread into triangles. Prick right through to the baking sheet with a fork in a neat pattern. Cover and chill for at least

1 hour before baking to firm it up.

3 Bake in the centre of a preheated oven, 150°C (300°F), Gas Mark 2, for 45–60 minutes, or until the shortbread is a pale biscuit colour but still soft. Remove from the oven and leave to cool and shrink before removing the ring, then dust lightly with caster sugar. When cold, store in an airtight tin.

Makes 6–8 pieces
Preparation time: 15 minutes, plus chilling
Baking time: 45–60 minutes
Oven temperature: 150°C (300°F), Gas Mark 2

Horseshoe Anniversary Cake

- 6 tablespoons apricot jam, sieved
- 1 kg/2 lb Fondant Moulding Paste (see page 89)
- 1-egg quantity Royal Icing (see page 88)
- 3 sprays of fresh orchids with foliage

1 x 5-EGG MADEIRA CAKE MIXTURE:

- 300 g/10 oz butter
- 300 g/10 oz caster sugar
- 300 g/10 oz self-raising flour
- 150 g/5 oz plain flour
- 5 eggs
- grated rind and juice of 2 lemons

1 Grease and line a 23 cm/9 inch horseshoe cake tin.

2 Make up the cake mixture as for Madeira cake (see page 44) and put into the prepared tin.

3 Bake in a preheated oven, 160°C (325°F), Gas Mark 3, for 1½–1¾ hours, or until a skewer inserted in the centre comes out clean.

4 Leave the cake to cool in the tin for about 10 minutes before turning out carefully on to a wire rack to cool completely.

5 Trim the cake off evenly at the base, if necessary, so that it sits flat on a cake board. Brush with the jam.

6 Roll out the Fondant Moulding Paste and use to cover the whole cake. Trim evenly around the base.

7 Immediately take a pair of curved icing crimpers and mark a crimped effect around the top edge of the cake. Leave to dry for 24 hours.

8 Put the Royal Icing into a paper icing bag, snip the end and pipe a snail's trail around the base.

9 Tie a large mauve ribbon around the sides of the cake securing it with a pin. Using fine icing wire, carefully wire the orchids and foliage together into a horseshoe shape and set them on top of the cake.

Makes one 23 cm/9 inch horseshoe-shaped cake

Preparation time: 3 hours, plus setting
Baking time: 1½–1¾ hours
Oven temperature: 160°C (325°F), Gas Mark 3

Aeroplane Cake

- 5 tablespoons apricot jam, sieved
- 4 long wooden skewers
- wooden cocktail sticks
- 1 kg/2 lb Fondant Moulding Paste (see page 89)
- liquid or paste food colourings – yellow, black and red
- black icing pen

2 x 5-EGG MADEIRA CAKE MIXTURE:
- 625 g/1¼ lb butter
- 625 g/1¼ lb caster sugar
- 625 g/1¼ lb self-raising flour
- 300 g/10 oz plain flour
- 10 eggs
- grated rind and juice of 4 lemons

1 Make up the cake mixture as for Madeira cake (see page 44). Grease and baseline two 20 x 30/8 x 12 inch cake tins.

2 Spoon the cake mixtures into the prepared tins and bake in a preheated oven, 160°C (325°F), Gas Mark 3, for about 1 hour. Let the cakes cool in the tins for about 10 minutes before turning on to wire racks to cool completely.

3 To make the body of the plane, cut off a long strip 7.5 cm/3 inches wide from one of the cakes. From the trimmings cut two tail wings and a tail tip. Cut a small piece slightly thinner than the body of the plane for the cockpit. Trim the back of the cockpit on the diagonal. Cut the second cake in half diagonally to form the wings.

4 Brush each piece of cake liberally with apricot jam and stick the wings to the body. Secure with long wooden skewers if necessary. Attach the small tail wings and the cockpit and secure as necessary with cocktail sticks. Carefully transfer the aeroplane to a cake board or serving platter.

5 Colour about 800 g/1 lb 12 oz Fondant Moulding Paste a bright yellow and roll out to a circle that is large enough to cover the plane completely. Using the palms of your hands lift the paste over the cake to cover it completely. Smooth the paste with your hands and trim with a knife.

6 Colour about 25 g/1 oz Fondant Moulding Paste black and roll out and stamp out three figure 8s (for the age of the child).

7 Colour 75 g/3 oz Fondant Moulding Paste red and cut out three zig-zag patterns plus a long red strip. Using a little water or jam stick the red shapes on to the wings and tail tip. Arrange the red strip around the base of the cockpit. Set the figure 8s on top of the zig-zags and make windows using the black icing pen. Leave to set.

Makes 1 cake

Preparation time: about 4 hours
Baking time: about 2 hours
Oven temperature: 160°C (325°F), Gas Mark 3

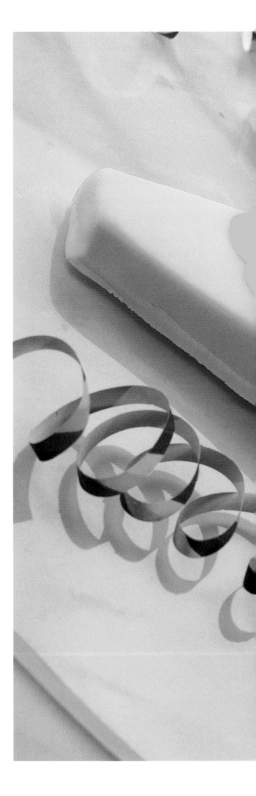

Pony Cake

- 4 tablespoons lemon curd
- 750 g/1½ lb Fondant Moulding Paste (see page 89)
- liquid or paste food colourings – blue, green, brown, black and red
- black and green icing pens
- chocolate matchstick sweets

4-EGG MADEIRA CAKE MIXTURE:

- 250 g/8 oz butter
- 250 g/8 oz caster sugar
- 250 g/8 oz self-raising flour
- 125 g/4 oz plain flour
- 4 eggs
- grated rind and juice of 1½ lemons

1 Grease and line a rectangular tin of about 20 x 30 x 4 cm/8 x 12 x 1½ inches with greased greaseproof paper or non-stick silicone paper.

2 Make up the cake mixture as for Madeira cake (see page 44) and put into the prepared tin, levelling the top and making sure there is plenty of mixture in the corners. Bake in a preheated oven, 160°C (325°F), Gas Mark 3, for 1–1¼ hours, or until well risen and firm to the touch.

3 Carefully turn out the cake on to a wire rack and leave until cold. Peel off the paper and trim off the top so the cake is even, then stand it on a suitably sized cake board or serving platter. Brush the cake all over with lemon curd.

4 Colour about 175 g/6 oz Fondant Moulding Paste a pale sky blue. Roll it out and place it over the top one-third or the cake, giving it a slightly uneven edge. Press over the cake evenly. Trim off neatly around the base of the cake.

5 Colour about 375 g/12 oz Fondant Moulding Paste a good grass green colour. Roll out and use to cover the rest of the cake, making it meet the sky evenly, and mould over the corners and down the sides of the cake. Trim off around the base of the cake.

6 Draw a picture of a horse jumping (or trace it from a picture) and put it on to a piece of thick paper or thin card. Cut it out neatly. Colour about 150 g/5 oz Fondant Moulding Paste brown and roll it out to a piece large enough to place the card on. Using a sharp knife, cut carefully around the template of the horse, then remove the template. Carefully pick up the horse and dampen the edges so the horse sticks to the cake.

7 Colour 25 g/1 oz Fondant Moulding Paste black and roll out thin strips to make the tail and mane. Attach with a little water.

8 Colour the remaining Fondant Moulding Paste red. Roll out thinly and cut out a 2.5 cm/1 inch circle and a 1 cm/½ inch circle and two thin streamers. Shape into a rosette and write '1st' on it with the black icing pen. Using a cocktail stick, frill the edges of the large circle to complete the rosette. Attach to the horse's neck.

9 Using chocolate matchsticks, make a post and rail fence and arrange under the horse.

10 Using the green icing pen, draw on grass. Using the black icing pen, make an eye, nostril and hooves on the pony. Leave to set overnight.

Makes one 20 x 30 x 4 cm/8 x 12 x 1½ inch cake

Preparation time: about 3 hours, plus cooling and setting

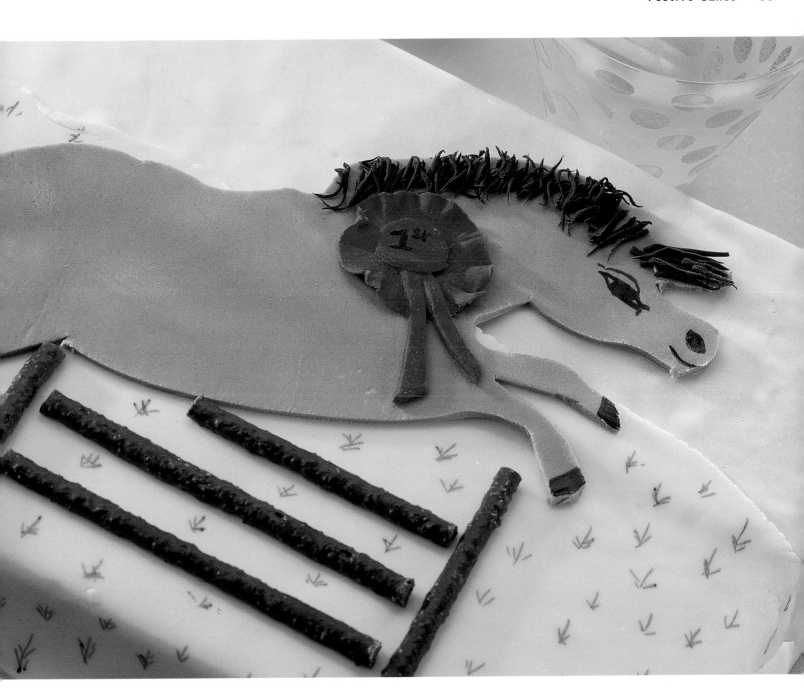

Baking time: about 1–1¼ hours
Oven temperature: 160°C (325°F),
Gas Mark 3

Coco the Clown Cake

1 x 5-EGG MADEIRA CAKE MIXTURE:

- 300 g/10 oz butter
- 300 g/10 oz caster sugar
- 300 g/10 oz self-raising flour
- 150 g/5 oz plain flour
- 5 eggs
- grated rind and juice of 2 lemons

1 x 3-EGG MADEIRA CAKE MIXTURE:

- 175 g/6 oz butter
- 175 g/6 oz caster sugar
- 175 g/6 oz self-raising flour
- 75 g/3 oz plain flour
- 3 eggs
- grated rind and juice of 1 lemon

CHOCOLATE BUTTER CREAM:

- 50 g/2 oz butter or margarine
- 75 g/3 oz icing sugar, sifted
- 25 g/1 oz cocoa powder, sifted
- a little milk
- 3 long wooden skewers
- 4 tablespoons apricot jam or marmalade, sieved
- 1 kg/2 lb Fondant Moulding Paste (see page 89)
- liquid or paste food colourings – peach, pink, yellow, red, orange, black and green
- 2 wooden cocktail sticks
- 1-egg quantity Royal Icing (see page 88)

1 Grease and line 3 round cake tins, 18, 15 and 12.5 cm/7, 6 and 5½ inch, with greased greaseproof paper or non-stick silicone paper. Grease a 600 ml/1 pint pudding basin, add a disc of non-stick silicone paper to the base and dust the basin lightly with flour.

2 Make up the two Madeira cake mixtures (see page 44). Divide the larger mixture between the largest and smallest cake tins, and the other mixture between the 15 cm/6 inch cake tin and the pudding basin, levelling all the tops evenly.

3 Bake in a preheated oven, 160°C (325°F), Gas Mark 3, allowing about 1¼ hours for the largest; 50–60 minutes for the middle and smallest cakes, and 45–50 minutes for the basin, until well risen, firm to the touch and a skewer inserted in the centre comes out clean. Cool briefly in the tins then turn out carefully on to wire racks and leave to cool. Leave for 12–24 hours to set before assembling.

4 To make up the Chocolate Butter Cream, cream the fat until soft then beat in the icing sugar and cocoa with sufficient milk to give a spreading consistency.

5 Build up the cakes into a clown, starting with the largest and attaching it to a 23 cm/9 inch round cake board with butter cream.

6 Spread the cake with butter cream and cover with the next cake. Again spread with butter cream and add the smallest cake. Trim off all the edges of the cakes to give an even, conical shape. Make a cut at the front of the cake at the base and remove a small wedge so that the cake is divided into two legs.

7 Trim off the base of the basin cake to make it more rounded for the head.

8 Attach the head to the body, again with butter cream, and then stick the 3 long wooden skewers down through the head and into the body and down through to the cake board. Brush all over the cake with jam.

9 Colour 175 g/6 oz of the Fondant Moulding Paste a flesh colour, roll out and use to cover the head, trimming off below the neck. Shape the trimmings into 2 large ears and 2 hands, marking fingers with a knife. Attach the ears to the head.

10 Colour 500 g/1 lb of the Fondant Moulding Paste a bright yellow. Roll out and cut into a semi-circle large enough to wrap round the body of the clown, trimming it off at the neck and joining it at the back. Also trim off around the base, pressing into the cut at the front for the legs.

11 Divide the yellow trimmings in half and mould each into an arm. Attach the hands to the ends of the arms and then attach them to the body with a cocktail stick and a dab of icing. Hold in place, if necessary, so they don't slip down.

12 Colour about 25 g/1 oz Fondant Moulding Paste a deep orange or red. First, mould a large red knob for a nose and attach it to the face then mould a large smiling mouth and 2 eyebrows.

13 Colour 125 g/4 oz Fondant Moulding Paste black and use to mould 2 long shoes and attach to the base of the cake at the bottom of the trousers. Roll out the remainder and cut out 1.5 cm/½ inch spots and attach them all over the clown's clothes.

14 Colour about 125 g/4 oz Fondant Moulding Paste a deep green colour and first cut out a bow tie. Roll out about a third of the remainder and cut into a circle about 6 cm/2½ inches in diameter. Roll the remainder into a ball with a flat base and attach to the hat with a dab of icing to make a bowler. Leave these to dry.

15 Cut out two large oval white clown eyes from the white fondant trimmings and a long oval for the mouth. Attach to the face with icing and then add the red mouth and eyebrows in the appropriate places.

16 Colour a tiny piece of Fondant Moulding Paste black and use to roll into 4 short sausages to make small crosses for eyes.

17 Put the Royal Icing into a piping bag fitted with a plain piping nozzle and pipe a ruff all round the neck of the clown. Attach the green bow tie at the front, then pipe a ruff around each wrist and at the bottom of the trousers. Pipe laces on to the shoes.

18 Colour a little icing orange and put into a piping bag fitted with a large plain piping nozzle. Use to pipe a few strands of hair down the back of the clown's head.

19 Finally, attach the bowler hat to the head of the clown at a jaunty angle and leave him to set for at least 24 hours.

Makes 1 cake

Preparation time: about 6 hours, plus cooling and setting
Cooking time: about 2½ hours
Oven temperature: 160°C (325°F), Gas Mark 3

Toppings and Fillings

Marzipan

300 g/10 oz ground almonds
300 g/10 oz caster sugar, sifted
2 egg yolks

2 tablespoons lemon or orange juice
a few drops of almond essence

1 Sift the ground almonds and sugar into a mixing bowl. Beat the egg yolks with the lemon or orange juice and stir into the dry ingredients. Work into a stiff paste and knead until smooth. The warmth of the hands brings out the oil in the ground almonds. If this makes the paste sticky, work in a little more sugar. If dry and crumbly, add a little more lemon or orange juice. If you are not using the the marzipan immediately, wrap it in clingfilm or foil and store in an airtight container for 2–3 days.

Makes enough to cover a 20 cm/8 inch round cake
Preparation time: 10 minutes

Royal Icing

- 3 egg whites
- 750 g/1½ lb icing sugar, sifted
- 3 teaspoons lemon juice, strained
- 1–1½ teaspoons glycerine (optional)

1 Put the egg whites into a clean bowl and beat until frothy. Using a wooden spoon, gradually beat in half of the icing sugar.

2 Add the lemon juice, glycerine, if using, and the remaining sugar 1 tablespoon at a time. Beat well until the mixture is smooth, very white and stands in soft peaks.

3 Transfer the icing to a sealed airtight container, or cover the bowl with a damp cloth to prevent a skin forming, and leave to stand for about 1 hour, to allow the air bubbles in the icing to disperse.

4 The icing is now ready to be used for coating a cake, or it can be thickened a little with extra sifted icing sugar to pipe stars, flowers and other decorations.

Makes 750 g/1½ lb icing
Preparation time: 10–15 minutes, plus standing

To Flat-ice a Cake ready for Decoration

1 Attach the cake to a cake board 2.5–5 cm/1–2 inches larger than the cake with a dab of icing, or place on an icing turntable. Put a quantity of icing on top of the cake and smooth out with a palette knife, using a paddling movement to dispel any remaining air bubbles and spread the icing out evenly.

2 Draw an icing ruler evenly across the top of the cake, holding it at an angle of about 30° and without exerting additional pressure.

3 Remove any surplus icing by running a palette knife round the top edge of the cake, holding it at right angles to the cake. Leave to dry.

4 Spread a thin covering layer of icing round the sides of the cake, again using a paddling movement.

5 Hold an icing comb or scraper at an angle of about 45° to the cake. Swivelling the cake on the turntable if using, or using your free hand to rotate it slowly, move the comb slowly and evenly round the sides of the cake. Remove the comb at an angle and fairly quickly, so the join is hardly noticeable.

6 Remove any excess icing from the top of the cake with a palette knife, again rotating the cake. Leave to dry.

Fondant Moulding Paste

- 500 g/1 lb icing sugar
- 1 egg white
- 50 g/2 oz liquid glucose or glucose syrup
- liquid or paste food colouring (optional)

1 Sift the icing sugar into a bowl and make a well in the centre.
2 Add the egg white and liquid glucose or glucose syrup. Beat with a wooden spoon, gradually drawing in the icing sugar from the side of the bowl, until the mixture is stiff.
3 Dip your hands into a mixture of icing sugar and cornflour, then knead the icing in the bowl, using the fingertips and kneading in a circular movement. Add food colouring sparingly, if using, and knead again until smooth and evenly coloured.
4 If not using immediately, store in a tightly sealed airtight container or sealed thick polythene bag for 2–3 days in a cool place.

Makes 500 g/1 lb
Preparation time: 10 minutes

To Cover a Cake with Fondant Moulding Paste

1 If the cake is covered with marzipan, brush lightly all over with egg white or leave it as it is. If the cake is uncovered, brush it all over with

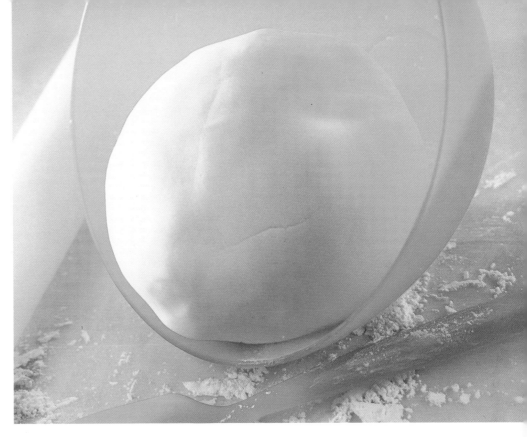

apricot glaze (see right).
2 Put a sheet of clingfilm or non-stick silicone paper on a work surface and dredge lightly with a mixture of cornflour and icing sugar. Roll out the fondant until it is 12–15 cm / 5–6 inches larger than the cake.
3 Support the icing on a rolling pin, drawing off the clingfilm if used, and position the icing centrally on top of the cake.
4 Dip your fingertips in a mixture of icing sugar and cornflour and press the icing over the sides of the cake, working from the centre to the edge, then down the sides, in a circular movement. Trim any excess icing from the base.
5 Leave for at least 24 hours and preferably 2–3 days to dry completely before decorating.

Apricot Glaze

- 125 g/4 oz apricot jam
- 1 tablespoon lemon juice
- 2 tablespoons water

1 Dissolve the jam thoroughly with the lemon juice and water in a small pan over gentle heat. When dissolved, boil until it drops off the edge of a wooden spoon in flakes. If the glaze is too liquid, it will not set.
2 Using a wooden spoon, strain the glaze through a wire sieve.

VARIATION

Redcurrant Glaze

Use redcurrant jelly instead of apricot jam. Do not overboil as it sets very quickly. It does not require sieving.

Pastry Cream

Also known as Crème Pâtissière, this is the classic French cream filling for cakes and pastries. For a slightly different version, pastry cream can also be flavoured with 1–2 tablespoons of fresh lemon juice or sweet sherry instead of vanilla or almond essence.

- **1 egg, plus 1 egg yolk**
- **50 g/2 oz caster sugar**
- **40 g/1½ oz flour**
- **300 ml/½ pint milk**
- **¼ teaspoon vanilla or almond essence**

1 Whisk the eggs and sugar together until smooth and nearly white. Gradually stir in the flour and then the milk. Pour into a small saucepan and bring to the boil, stirring steadily. Simmer for 3–5 minutes, stirring, to cook the flour thoroughly.
2 If a thick cream is required, cook for a few minutes longer to reduce the liquid.
3 Flavour to taste with vanilla or almond essence and pour into a cold dish to cool. Stir from time to time to prevent a skin forming.

Makes about 300 ml/½ pint
Preparation time: 5 minutes
Cooking time: 3–5 minutes

Little Cakes

These little cakes are quick and easy to make and equally good topped with Glacé Icing (see right and pages 92 and 93) or Butter Cream (see page 95).

- 250 g/8 oz plain flour
- pinch of salt
- 1½ teaspoons baking powder
- 75 g/3 oz butter or margarine
- 50–75 g/2–3 oz sugar
- 1 egg, beaten
- about 75 ml/3 fl oz milk or water
- glacé icing, to decorate

1 Sift the flour, salt and baking powder into a mixing bowl. Cut the butter or margarine into the flour and rub in to a breadcrumb consistency. Mix in the sugar thoroughly.

2 Using a fork, stir in the egg and sufficient milk or water to give a stiff consistency – the fork should stand up in the dough.

3 Spoon the mixture in little heaps or small balls on a greased baking sheet or in bun tins and bake near the top of a preheated oven, 220–230°C (425–450°F), Gas Mark 7–8, for 10–15 minutes.

4 Cool on a wire rack. When cold, decorate with glacé icing or butter cream.

Makes 12–16

Preparation time: 5–10 minutes, plus cooling
Baking time: 10–15 minutes
Oven temperature: 220–230°C (425–450°F), Gas Mark 7–8

Glacé Icing

- about 1 tablespoon water
- 125 g/4 oz icing sugar, sifted
- flavouring (see below)

1 Stir the water into the icing sugar very gradually, and mix to a spreading consistency, adding a little more water if necessary. Beat until smooth. For a thinner icing, mix to a pouring consistency, adding ½ teaspoon water at a time. For a very thin, transparent icing continue adding the water very carefully. Flavour and colour to taste (see below).

Chocolate
Sift 1 tablespoon cocoa powder with the icing sugar and mix with black coffee instead of water.

Coffee
Sift 2 teaspoons instant coffee powder with the icing sugar and mix with black coffee instead of water.

Lemon
Mix with strained lemon juice instead of water. Tint pale yellow with a few drops of yellow colouring, or leave white.

Lemon curd
Beat 3–4 teaspoons lemon curd with the basic mixture.

Orange
Use orange juice instead of water to mix, and tint with a few drops of orange colouring, if liked.

Peppermint
Add a few drops of peppermint oil to the basic mixture and tint a delicate green, if liked.

Vanilla
Add a few drops of vanilla essence to the basic mixture and tint pink with a few drops of cochineal, if liked.

Butter Cream

125 g/4 oz unsalted butter
- **175 g/6 oz icing sugar, sifted**
- **flavouring (see below)**

1 Cream the butter and gradually beat in the icing sugar until smooth. Flavour and colour as required in one of the ways suggested below.

Chocolate
Sift 1 tablespoon cocoa powder with the icing sugar and add ¼ teaspoon vanilla essence or a little rum.

Coffee
Sift 1–2 teaspoons instant coffee powder with the icing sugar.

Mocha
Sift 2 teaspoons instant coffee powder and 1 tablespoon cocoa powder with the icing sugar.

Lemon
Cream the finely grated rind of
1 lemon with the butter and add
1–2 teaspoons lemon juice to the
butter cream. Tint with a few drops of
yellow colouring, if liked.

Lemon curd
Beat 2 tablespoons lemon curd with
the basic mixture.

Orange
Cream the finely grated rind of
1 orange with the butter and add
1 tablespoon orange juice to the butter
cream. Tint with a few drops of orange
colouring, if liked.

Raspberry
Beat 2–3 tablespoons raspberry jam
into the basic mixture and sharpen to
taste with lemon juice. Tint pink with
a few drops of cochineal, if liked.

Walnut
Beat 2–3 tablespoons ground walnuts
into the basic mixture.

Recipe photographers:
Reed International Books Ltd./
Bryce Attwell/Gina Harris/
RogerPhillips/Simon Smith/
Paul Williams
Jacket Photographer:
Simon Smith
Jacket Home Economists
Lucy Knox and Sarah Lowman